Balboa Press books may be ordered through booksellers or by contacting:

Balboa Press
A Division of Hay House
1663 Liberty Drive
Bloomington, IN 47403
www.balboapress.com
1 (877) 407-4847

Print information available on the last page.

ISBN: 978-1-9822-0501-0 (sc)
ISBN: 978-1-9822-0502-7 (e)

Balboa Press rev. date: 05/30/2018

July
2020
Dear Silva,
May you the
reach
Self-love
solution.
xo
Grace

SO YOU LOVE AN . . .

Alcoholic?

LESSONS FOR A CODEPENDENT

GRACE W. WROLDSON

BALBOA
PRESS
A DIVISION OF HAY HOUSE

for my child,
and for all the children
of this dilemma

A special thanks to my sponsor

DISCLAIMER

My story is written in a pen name to protect the anonymity of all involved. I do not name the alcoholic. From my understanding, alcoholism is generally a socially, self-diagnosed disease within the Twelve-Steps Support Groups. Therefore, I am not diagnosing the alcoholic condition but rather confessing my matching codependency condition that I self-identified. I refer to the Al-Anon/ACA Twelve-Step Family Groups as *my recovery* and *my program*.

Originally, the alcoholic was "my qualifier" that led me to seek help by attending Twelve-Step meetings. Over my years in these meetings, I realized that I was actually my own "qualifier" with issues of reacting, controlling, and suffering an attachment disorder. I was taught, by my family, that alcoholism is a family disease, thus I refer to the disease more often than the alcoholic. I repeat this phrase throughout the book to emphasize this point. By repeating "alcoholic" and "disease of alcoholism," I remind myself and my readers that their partners are suffering as well. It is also a way to affirm that the disease of alcohol is to blame, not so much the person. It will be noted that I repeat myself, saying the same thing in a slightly different way, because repetition is the key to learning. The way I learned my lessons was by repeating these truths.

Furthermore, I try to show the separation of the alcoholic from this disease, to make clear a distinction. Sometimes, I purposefully say "my alcoholic" rather than say "the alcoholic" because not every alcoholic is the same. Saying it this way, is not meant to be an ownership of the alcoholic as mine or belonging to me (which I used to do in my sickness), but rather pointing out that this was my situation – with a unique individual, and a complex issue. This is my interpretation of recovering from the effects of alcoholism. Take what lesson you like and leave the rest, perhaps for another time.

Contents

Stage I
The Very Codependent Caterpillar

Stage II
In the Cocoon of New Creation

Stage III
Becoming and Being a Beautiful Butterfly
(Taking Flight)

Stage IV

About This Book

Lesson: Be Open to Learning the Lessons

"You were born with wings,
Why prefer to crawl through life?"
— *Jalāl ad-Dīn Muhammad Rūmī*

✧ So you love an alcoholic?

✧ Are you a woman who loves an alcoholic man?

✧ Are you a woman who has spent years trying to love a man who drinks?

✧ Do you want to stop your very unhealthy, toxic love and codependent ways?

✧ Are you ready to leave, heal, and live again?

This book is for women who seek healing within this very challenging subject. In order to heal, I had to learn my lessons, name them, and allow them to change me. I discovered that in order to change my life and not repeat my past with an alcoholic man, I had to make changes within myself. This book is intended for those women who are ready to courageously place themselves in the center of their own lives. My question to you is, "I know you love him, but isn't it time to love yourself more?"

I ask you the same questions I asked myself:

◇ Does life with his drinking (and his thinking) no longer appeal to you?
◇ Are you feeling stuck, hopeless, and in despair?
◇ Would you like to break the spell that the alcoholic seems to have over you?
◇ Are ready to set yourself free from a life of coping and dealing with his drinking?
◇ Do you want to be happy?

In this brave book, I share the conversation that my soul had with itself. I went through pain, shame, and failure. This book contains the collected wisdom I gained through educating myself on alcoholism, codependency, and love addiction. I added up my knowledge, my personal experiences, plus my personal recovery in Al-Anon, and my own self-help studies, and out came this wisdom that I wish I had discovered years ago. Here, I journaled my journey out of my "codependent-crazies."

I was inspired by the story, *The Very Hungry Caterpillar* by Eric Carle, a children's book that I read to my daughter countless times. To me, the butterfly is a magical being. Personally, I could relate to the process of undergoing a change —of that magnitude. I could see myself and my life played-out similar to that colorful story. When I started loving an alcoholic, I myself was a very hungry, codependent caterpillar! Like the caterpillar, I crawled along the ground looking for food and easy meals, which I equate to the loneliness of looking for relief from the pain of being in an alcoholic relationship. When I was finally tired of crawling along the ground and eventually gathered the strength to leave the relationship, I needed time to reflect and heal. I isolated myself in a cocoon of sorts which I call my chrysalis. Finally, after several years warming in the light of the sun, in sacred solitude, nurturing myself and allowing a Higher Power to change me, I eventually emerged as a beautiful butterfly! I emerged with wings, free to live my own life and fly. Success stories, like that of a caterpillar to a butterfly, satisfy my soul. I love a dirt-to-diamonds story of transformation, especially my own. How one can go from crawling on the ground to flying in the air is a miraculous mystery. I must add that learning how to fly wasn't easy, but it sure is better than codependently crawling!

These passages, these words, can help you navigate the stages of personal change. Some emotionally difficult phases are involved with the transformation process. The breakdown of the caterpillar, isolated in the cocoon, had to happen. Pain is part of the process. As I went through —and survived— each stage, I witnessed the phases of my change much like that of a soon-to-be-butterfly.

My Lesson: Learn my lessons!

I write about my insights. I write about my newfound awarenesses. I write about my spiritual awakenings. I share my beginning, my middle, and my end (including my maintenance phase) of my very personal journey of loving an alcoholic man and leaving him behind. These are my codependent confessions.

You might read all of my Stage I, where I crawled around in my mind trying to feed my thoughts something healthy (Stage I: Every End is a New Beginning - Crawling on the Ground Craving a Companion). Or you may skip to Stage II, the section where I cocooned myself and started my deep inner-work (Stage II: In the Cocoon of New Creation - The Chrysalis of Change). Or you may really want to hear my Stage III lessons when I emerged a brilliant butterfly (Stage III: Becoming and Being a Beautiful Butterfly - Taking Flight). Or perhaps you want to connect with Stage IV on how I learned to live again (Stage IV: Flying with Brilliance and Grace - Dancing the Dance of Life - From a Higher Altitude).

Sitting in an isolated corner of the local coffee shop, which I consider my cocoon, I originally wrote these passages as a journal to myself. Like an enclosed butterfly, I captured my imaginal cells.

(Imaginal cells are dormant cells within the chrysalis containing poetic genius that help the process of creating a new form and structure.) I discovered that writing was very therapeutic. Journaling was how I reset and rewired my brain to correct my faulty codependent thinking; it was my chrysalis. Reading back through my journals is how I remembered my lessons. Reading them many times was what made me aware of my metamorphosis.

You will read how being touched by the disease of alcoholism pushed me to grow and create new and better thoughts that brightened my future. Codependency and love addiction were my battles to fight while alcohol was one of the alcoholic's battles that I couldn't fight for him. I fought an internal war, and in the end, I learned how to surrender to each stage to necessitate change.

By seeing my strength take shape on this subject, you may acquire some courage of your own to begin the stages of changing your life. I continue to live and lead as proof that you can live on with wisdom to lead a fuller, richer, and more authentic life. There is a way to survive toxic codependency and the often deadly disease of alcoholism. Once you have survived it, I believe you can then thrive from it. Practicing recovery filled me with my own power, self-love, and serenity. Maintaining those gifts takes one day at a time. Are you open to learning your lessons? Will my story of survival help you?

"And the day came when
the risk to remain tight in a bud
was more painful
than the risk it took to blossom."
— Anaïs Nin

About the Author

Grace Wroldson spent fifteen years of her precious life loving an alcoholic. Almost marrying him, she was in and out of the relationship, struggling to escape her active alcoholic while battling her codependency issues. For years she attempted to save him and save the relationship by studying the disease of alcoholism and learning from the Twelve Step Recovery groups of AA, ACOA, and Al-Anon. When the alcoholic did not choose sobriety nor recovery in AA, she empowered herself to leave the long-term unhealthy, toxic relationship. She went into recovery in Al-Anon. She equipped herself with recovery tools, learned her lessons, and labeled them. With her focus on herself, she was able to strengthen her self-esteem which grew into a better life, a life with self-love.

To the surprise of everyone, life gave her a parting gift of an unexpected child three months after the final break-up with the alcoholic. Still having to deal with the alcoholism while raising a child safely, with the disease close at her heels, she chose to change herself and work her recovery program harder than ever in order to save two lives.

Now, with 20 years of recovery knowledge and wisdom, she shares her story of triumph. She is committed to empowering other women to courageously place themselves in the center of their own lives, too. She changed her dark destiny and shifted her life to a faith-filled future. By placing bold boundaries and opting-out of painful situations she sought a healthier relationship with herself and found a Higher Power. Her story serves as a woman's lighthouse light and paves the road for other women to perform the same act of saving grace.

Synopsis of My Love Story

"She let go...
She let go of all the "right" reasons.
Wholly and completely, without hesitation or worry, she just let go...
There was no applause or congratulations.
No one thanked her or praised her...
It was what it was, and it is just that."
— Rev. Safire Rose; She Let Go

One woman's story of tragedy to triumph loving an alcoholic.

My beginning, end, and rebirth...

Have you ever loved a man so much and felt such a connection in your soul that you placed him on the stage of your life and then built your dreams around him? For me, that man was the most handsome boy in my high school. I had placed a spotlight on him; he was my star. He had everything going for him. When he spoke, his words were music to my ears. Of all the girls in school, I felt lucky that he had chosen me. The alcoholic I fell in love with was a prize to be won, or so I thought.

In reality, he was my great love gone wrong. My future life with him turned out much differently than what I had hoped, dreamed, and expected. Discouraging days and nights dragged on into disappointing years. The alcoholic's directionless decade of drinking dampened his glow yet I still kept my spotlight on him. I still clung to him and stood by - watching and waiting — hoping he would change into the man I believed he could be. I loved him so much, I hurt. I suffered right alongside him, subjecting myself to years of betrayal, confusion, and deep-seated depression. The effects of alcoholism took a toll on my self-esteem. Somewhere in the romance, I turned over my self-worth. Somehow, I became a co-addicted, codependent woman.

Fifteen years slipped by before I finally garnered enough courage to leave on my own terms, but in order to leave this love, I had to break my own heart. That's when my real work, and this book, began. Through a twist of fate, I found out I was pregnant three months after I left the alcoholic. My misfortune was that as soon as real responsibility showed up, he was not able to be the man I hoped he would be, nor the man he claimed he was all those years. His words turned out to be just words but with no music. My great love for him was gone with the click of my apartment door when he said something to me that made my heart sink to my stomach.

With enough recovery in the Twelve-Step Program of Al-Anon, I did what I knew was right — I turned my love and attention to my unborn child and away from the alcoholic. I vowed for her to never see the darkness and destruction of the disease in our home. I loved her before she even arrived. By practicing recovery, by helping myself, and by relying on the kindness of strangers, I raised our child on my own to be safe and strong against this adversary. With my new strength, the alcoholic lost his power over me. I became free. Free again to love myself.

Letting go of the alcoholic felt like a death. I had to grieve the loss of the relationship. While the alcoholic was not literally deceased, he was spiritually dead to me. My soul sustained the loss of love that I had slowly been losing with my co-sickness. The disease of alcoholism was progressive; it took everything. I saw him diminish in every way a man possibly can, short of the grave. I saw myself fall apart in a separate type of graveyard for battered, codependent souls.

However, with recovery, separated from the alcoholic, I began to grow. I began to blossom with a baby in my belly. My great love for her kept me strong. Through daily amends to myself, I began to forgive myself for the messy life circumstances that I tied myself to and that I brought my child into. Through ongoing recovery and learning my lessons, I turned my fate into fortunate circumstances. I survived and saved my life. I triumphed over this tragedy. My grief transformed into gratitude. I single-handedly built a new platform, and I stepped onto the stage of the life I wanted to be living.

With my life as my stage, I became my own star. I turned my ear to my own voice and listened to my own words of wisdom. I even dared to dream new dreams and rebuild my life towards them and around myself (this time) as a solid foundation. I was about to give birth to a baby girl and a new version of me at the same time. I poured my love into her precious awaiting soul. I wrote my lessons down and loved them. Eventually, I started loving myself with an even greater love than I had for the alcoholic.

In Loving Memory

In loving memory of my grandfather, D.W., who reached recovery, joined AA, found God, practiced the Program, changed his life, made direct amends, shared his miracle, served others, and carried the message to suffering alcoholics up to his last day. Grandpa, I am proud of you for living and dying sober. You are an inspiration to me. Thank you for showing me that recovery can happen. Men can change. Recovery does work, if you work it. Miracle life makeovers do happen. Attending your funeral and seeing those that you helped to stay sober, showed me that, by changing ourselves for the better, we can make a difference in other's lives. We live and we touch. You demonstrated that we get many chances to pay the goodness of our recovery forward. I have all your gold anniversary coins for each year that you celebrated sobriety in AA. I celebrate your accomplishment. You pointed the way when you said to me, "Honey, you're sicker than the alcoholic!" You were right. Thank you for telling me the truth. I found recovery, too. May you rest in peace.

In Loving Prayer:

In loving prayer for the alcoholic man who I loved all those years. I will continue to do the best thing I can for you... detach with love and pray.

In loving prayer for our child in an alcoholic situation. Dear One, may you be strong with the fortified foundation of recovery I have set forth. May this recovery immunize you from harm. May my miracle and my new choices bless us both.

In loving prayer *for me*, as I have learned to pray for myself. May the self-love solution sustain me all the rest of my days.

Amen.

I Walked Away

I walk away, soul battered and bruised,
I walked away with no more fight left in me,
I walked away with my list of failures and defeats,
I walked away with a heavy, hurting heart,
I walked away not knowing where to walk.

I walked away too tired to talk,
I walked away only to sit down for a year, in pain and shame,
What I didn't know was that I didn't walk away alone,
I walked away with a secret, silent blessing in my belly,
I walked away walking with an invisible creator at my side.

What I did was...
I walked away from him
and then I walked toward a new me.

— Grace Wroldson

Lesson: We Have Rights

Welcome Women!
(One woman's welcome to another)

"Walking, I am listening to a deeper way.
Suddenly all my ancestors are behind me.
Be still, they say. Watch and listen.
You are the result of the love of thousands."
— Linda Hogan

So you love an alcoholic? Welcome to my world, and the world of so many other women who have walked before us. For hundreds of years, let me say... most likely thousands of years, women have been suffering this exact same dilemma — a drunken husband! I believe that the dilemma of the drunken husband was what pushed American women to stand up for themselves, to separate themselves from their husband's ownership, and to ultimately seek the right to vote. When we walk this path, we walk with a thousand ancestors behind us.

I came to this theory when I was sitting outside the first home and birthplace of Susan B. Anthony, an honorable woman, and an American hero who fought for women's rights. I discovered a tiny fact that has impacted my life so greatly. A fact that was buried in bloomers of all places (that's right— those baggy pants for women)!

Two years ago, I sat with my young daughter on Miss Anthony's lawn, listening to a children's story and participating in fun historical kids' activities. To my astonishment, the historian read a line from a children's book that made a connection between bloomers and alcohol. Shocked to hear such a thing, I looked down at my child with my eyes wide. As the historian kept reading the book out loud to us, my mind raced and began to connect the dots. History is a powerful teacher.

When I got home, I rushed to verify the information and do more research on women's reasons for requesting voting rights in 1920. I discovered that part of the drive behind the 19th Amendment to the U.S. Constitution was that women wanted freedom from a drunken husband! During that time, this was known as temperance. How could I have missed the meaning of this term (temperance) after studying alcoholism for twenty years? As their first right, women wanted husbands to refrain from drunkenness! But first, they needed rights, especially the right to vote.

You might imagine my shock, because my child and I were sitting there, free of an alcoholic (loving our life of temperance) with equal rights, and the right to vote — that sunny day. We were actually living Susan's dream and hope for us. Seeing this dream come to fruition, which would have seemed like a huge fantasy to women in the 1800s, was awe-inspiring. My life of freedom from a drunken husband was owed to a great woman that I will never be able to meet or thank, so I made it my mission to honor her goals (in my own life) and build upon the foundation she put in place (for me and all women). Unknowingly, I walked into an alcoholic relationship; then I walked out of the alcoholic situation, and thanks to her fight for me, I was free to walk away. That was my vote.

Through my research, I learned that women's rights, voting, and temperance were all tied together. Miss Anthony died in 1906, but her mission continues to be carried out. She did not live to see women get the right to vote in 1920, but I think she knew our destiny. That day, filled with gratitude and tears, I felt like I was given a new set of eyes with which to see, a bigger vision of what my life was about to become, and a sense of how big my story was about to be for all of women's history. I was living in the transition time of gaining my rights and using my rights. I was living in the space and time it takes to not just realize that I have rights but live with my rights always in mind. Times were changing.

Telling my story

When I decided to break my silence on the subject of loving an alcoholic, by writing my book, startling coincidences began to happen. For instance, when I received an invitation from the town's historical society in the mail, it felt synchronistic.

It read:

"In 2020, the United States will celebrate the 100th anniversary of the 19th amendment giving women the right to vote. That same year marks the 200th birthday of our famous daughter, Susan B. Anthony. Help us give Adams the recognition it deserves as the birthplace of Susan, who is a nationally recognized leader in the women's movement."

A tribute to Susan B. Anthony

"Independence is happiness." —*Susan B. Anthony*

From that incredibly well-timed invitation, with my book, and with the freedom Miss Anthony gave me, I plan to give her some more recognition she deserves. I also plan to recognize a thousand-year-old-problem that our ancestral women have faced and we still face today. Surely, this invitation was a 100-year-old confirmation card sent from the past to the present, letting me know that I was on the right path. Has it only been 100 years since we've had the right to vote?

Initially, I had some doubts that this book would be of value to women. However, when I received the invitation, it convinced me that my story was important. (You might imagine my relief, because I had already written half of my book on loving and leaving an alcoholic.) Right then, my book became as much about welcoming other women in a similar situation and sharing with them my lessons, as it became about recognizing women's rights with a new historical artifact. My book is intended for women who want to heal from an alcoholic relationship, but first women must remember their rights and how we established them. Our history is important.

"There is not a woman born who desires to eat the bread of dependence, no matter whether it be from the hand of father, husband, or brother; for anyone who does so eat her bread places herself in the power of the person from whom she takes it."
— Susan B. Anthony

I imagine that in her hometown of Adams, Massachusetts, the pioneer of women's rights, Susan B. Anthony, must have known a woman (or two) who was locked in the unfortunate circumstances of being married to an alcoholic man with no right to own property or to escape legally. (Yes, women could not own property, nor could they legally be guardians of their own children in the event of a husband's passing, nor in a divorce prior to 1920.) I also assume that alcohol and alcoholic husbands made this even more of a challenge. Do we take our rights for granted today? Coincidently, didn't prohibition come shortly after women gained the right to vote? Are you connecting the dots, too?

Lesson: We are not alone

With or without knowing it, Miss Anthony fought the fight for our freedom, from the disease of alcoholism. She dedicated her life to the vote for women and won rights for us. From her great accomplishment, I believe we must carry out the rest of our rights regarding this freedom by the way we choose to live. Our ancestors knew what women of these circumstances were up against, and they must have known the accompanying social shame, emotional pain, disappointment, and legal complications. Miss Anthony was a hero for women when she displayed the courage to give speeches, during those days, and spoke up on our behalf. She was an ancestor who walked before us and who I believe is still walking with us.

On that sunny day, I learned two important things which have supported my mission to share my story:

1. I have rights.
2. I am not alone.

We women can now legally and constitutionally claim our right to live free of the drunkenness. We can exercise our right to live free of alcohol in all its horrible forms and aftermath. We can cast a vote in our own private lives or homes, and we can keep our homes. We have our rights. We can now choose to exercise that right if we find our life and home drowning from alcohol or drugs. We can exorcise ourselves from those situations and be our own hero.

I honor our women heroes who have gone before us. I honor Susan B. Anthony. It will take more of us great women to accomplish the use of this amendment by using it in our lives. Let all of us women who are faced with the problem of alcoholism in our homes be the heroine in our life! Remember, we are not alone. We walk our walk with our female ancestors backing us and with so many other women alongside us. If we women are going to walk, let's walk with wisdom.

"Above all, be the heroine of your life, not the victim."
— *Nora Ephron, Commencement Address to Wellesley Class of 1996*

My Prayer

I pray for the man I love,
And I pray for the man I hate.

My Blessing to You

May this book be a blessing to all the women who actively love an active alcoholic.

May this book and my "story wisdom" walk with you as you step through your own story.

May this book share the message (of transformation) and not just the mess (of troubles).

May you have hope.
May you come to courageously place yourself
at the center of your own life.
May you be the hero you have been waiting for.
May you come to a greater understanding of
yourself in relationship to alcoholism.
May you learn that codependency is not love, but fear.
May you conquer the fear of taking responsibility
for yourself and making a mistake.
May you continuously grant yourself permission to focus on you.
May you find a version of a loving Higher Power
to lead and light your way.
May you get into alignment with
a Higher Power's will for you and the Real You.
May you find an inner serenity and the peace
that only You and a Higher Power can provide.
May you finally be free to live your own life on your own terms.
May you learn ways to love yourself daily.
May you heal at the deepest level and at the center of your being.
May you listen to and hear your own complete
thoughts, words, and intuition.
May you honor your soul's calling and messages.
May you discover your choices.
May you transform your pain.
May you handle the truth gracefully.
And may you handle Reality truthfully.
May you grow spiritually and discover a fulfilling spiritual life.
May you find yourself and never get lost again.

My Desperation

I sold my soul,
Now, I want to buy it back.
From who, from where, from when?
I've lost years of track.
Yes, I'll admit, I've lost myself along the way.
I gave up parts of myself to what any man would say,
I've bargained whole pieces of me, I dare to say.
I'm ashamed to confess, that I even threw most of me away!
All of me I lost, to survive the pain and loneliness of that day,
So here now I sit, in my sad and sorry truth of today,
For I cannot see, hear, feel, or know my way.
— Grace Wroldson

Introduction

Question to my readers...

Have you suffered enough?

"Pain is inevitable. Suffering is optional."
— *Haruki Murakami*

✧ Does the drinking bother you?
✧ Are you sick and tired of being sick and tired?
✧ Do you want to live again?

When I first asked myself these questions, every cell in my body screamed, "Yes!" "Yes, I have suffered enough!" At rock bottom (a soul destroyed place), enough was enough for me! My relationship with the alcoholic and his relationship with alcohol had become so bad that even my body started yelling at me. I experienced not just emotional pain but also physical pain. I was suffering.

If you are tired of the insanity, if you have finally admitted and have come to the conclusion that you, too, have suffered enough, if you feel an urge to run away or wake up as a new person, then this book is for you. May it give you strength and reassurance to know that some of us romantic-type women have gone before you on this road of loving an alcoholic. Some of us have paved our own way through the pain, uncertainty, and fear. Grab ahold of your life vest (this book) if you feel it is time for you to jump from his sinking ship and onto the shore to save yourself! Please note: swimming skills are required!

I share my personal story with you with the hope and intention that it offers you insights into your story of loving an alcoholic. Almost all of the lessons of loving an alcoholic took place in the depths of my understandings of myself. Sometimes other people's stories have a way of shedding new light on our own. I think it is important to mention the obvious—that every love story is different, unique, and diverse. What absolutely worked for me may in no universe ever work for you. What worked for other women, for instance, getting immediately remarried to a healthier man, didn't work for me. However, more importantly, I discovered what did work for me. I would love for you to discover your own solutions, too!

A word of caution:

As you read my story, please take what you need and leave the rest for if/when you might need it. This book is meant to be a validating message of hope for you. I do not give specific advice about your alcoholic relationship other than to let my story help you to begin or continue your healing process. I was the author of my life story, and you and your Higher Power (if you have spiritual beliefs) are the coauthors of yours.

In your unique situation of loving an alcoholic, I ask that you use caution, as well as supportive, safe people and your best "survival smarts" because of the sometimes-abusive nature of the active alcoholic, especially when they are drinking. Alcoholic relationships can and often do include violence. I suggest that women seek several supports for themselves and children. I took advantage of all the support agencies available, which included Al-Anon, private therapy, financial assistance programs, church funds, domestic violence and abuse counseling services, police, free legal aid, etc. On top of all that outer support, I went for inner support. I read many, many books on the subject of alcoholism, codependency, and love addiction to educate and protect myself.

I don't advocate ending relationships, nor do I advise women to continue to be in a relationship with an active alcoholic. I agree that those decisions are best left to each woman to make with support. (Again, I will reiterate "if and when" any of these lessons may apply to you.) I do, however, emphasize taking the personal responsibility of taking care of yourself. I understand the need for basic survival in this situation. I had to take care of myself and manage my life, whether in or out of the relationship with an alcoholic. I understand that each relationship comes with surrounding circumstances that may include housing issues and children. All the factors in an alcoholic relationship need to be considered with caution. I used caution.

Another word of caution regarding quick solutions:

In my early recovery, I struggled with what I call "man solutions." These were not sustainable solutions for me at all. When you stop obsessing about the alcoholic, do you immediately start dreaming-up or daydreaming about another man? Do you mistakenly get caught thinking that what you really need is rescuing from this alcoholic relationship by another, richer, better man who doesn't drink?

I found that switching men was a lot like moving to Florida... I still took "sick little me" along to the new state. I still had the same sickness of codependency in my suitcases. As soon as I unpacked, there my problems were again! The love addict inside of me was looking for another hit. So was my problem really the alcoholic?

I ask you... What would it take for you to be the hero in your own life? Do you have a place in your heart for yourself? Is it your turn to be on the stage of your life, rather than revolving around a man that you put a spotlight on? For me, I had to do a "man-detox" that went beyond eating celery, drinking water, and avoiding online-dating websites. I had to know, be told, and tell myself that this was my life and my life was my stage! I had to come to realize that I was the hero I was waiting for!

> *"Just keep coming home to yourself, you are the one who you've been waiting for."*
> — *Byron Katie*

Would it shock you to discover that you are the one you've been waiting for all this time? That perhaps you haven't been waiting for the alcoholic to stop drinking and become the love of your life? Ultimately, you call yourself to change the life you are living. I believe that we have an internal mechanism that can indeed call to us. My inner voice went from a whisper to a yell. When I got healthier within the alcoholic relationship, I heard it cry out at times, and sometimes I was able to push through my fears to answer the call. It's called the Hero's Journey.

My math equations for a better life:

I subscribe to the theory that your "insides" create your "outsides." Better said, your inner life affects your outer life and perception of life. What's happening inside of you often creates what's happening outside of you. I have also heard it said a different way —that our personality creates our personal reality. Well... any way it's said, I believe it to be true. I have seen my personality and insides projected into my life. As my insides changed, as I healed, as I got better, I began to demand a different respect out of life, myself, and the alcoholic. When my mind, body, and spirit became healthier, my life circumstances around me adjusted and also became healthier. If you agree that this is true, this means that at any moment, whenever you are ready (on the inside), you can start living a better life than a trapped existence in an alcoholic relationship. My mental math began...

My insides = My perceptions

My outside life = My inside life

I found ways to change and push through my resistance. Of course, I needed, used, and accepted a huge amount of help. It's important to note that I learned that "being ready" didn't just mean ready and able to support myself financially, but that I also had to be ready to endure the difficult grieving process, as well as to endure intense bouts of relationship withdrawal. I had to begin emotionally supporting myself. Then I had to pass the loneliness "test" several times. I had to use the "finding myself again" factor in my math equation for a happy life.

Knowledge of him and myself +
Experiences that I had with him and being me
= My Wisdom

My wisdom applied to my life + Help + A healed version of me
= A Better Life

Better Life = Happier Me

The biggest multiplier (something that helped me the most) in my math equations for my escape from the relationship with the alcoholic was "story medicine." I was hearing hundreds of women's stories of love, pain, loss, and survival in the Twelve-Step Program of Al-Anon. Recovery in these program support groups and getting doses of "story medicine" became my strength and ongoing support through the hard times. I found my own answers to surviving and leaving the long-term toxic relationship — for good! Recovery from codependency sickness required my full commitment and complete immersion into Al-Anon, plus other popular and effective self-help strategies. I literally rescued myself with recovery and helped myself through my own story. You can, too!

Sitting in meetings + Listening to other women's stories = More wisdom to apply to my life

I turned hating myself and my life into loving myself and my life. I went from being hard on myself for mistakes to being gentle with my own humanness. I discovered that I was more fragile than I knew, yet at the same time, stronger than I had imagined. There was a way I needed to learn my life's lessons. Sometimes, well… probably oftentimes, I required learning the same lessons over and over just to be sure my old solutions of loving him wouldn't work. I had to nail my lessons down on paper. I had to look at my fear, anger, jealousy, and rage. I had to confess my expectations of this man. Not only did I have to face those mental monsters, but I also had to meet them, greet them, and show them the door!

Fear + Fear Faced + Breathing + Self-Compassion + Program Friends + A Higher Power = Courageous Acts

Loving an alcoholic man was not easy. The only thing harder than loving him was leaving him. Being involved with him was a major burden and barrier to living to my full potential. My involvement with him and his dilemma took up most of my life. The involvement I had with him took its toll on me emotionally, mentally, and physically. At my personal bottom (at my lowest) with the alcoholic, it became about knowing when to walk away and forcing myself to finally act on my own behalf. I had to repeat the phrase "I will not self-sabotage!" whenever I was dealing with him.

Year after year, it became clear; this man I loved, the alcoholic, simply would not get help. In the simplest sense, the decision was therefore made. He made a decision not to get help. I had to make a different decision in response. I knew I had to leave. I had to get the help he wouldn't get. I had to get the help he said he didn't need. I had to get the help that I stubbornly thought I didn't need. There came a relationship mile-marker: when it became clear to me that the only thing harder for me than leaving the alcoholic was trying to stay with him! I faced the pain of change, and similarly, I faced the pain of never changing. I chose to change.

**Self-Love + Self-Approval + Self-Affirmations
+ Recovery + Spiritual Solutions
= My ability to leave the alcoholic relationship**

If you have already made the decision to leave or have left and are suffering with self-doubt, this book can help you keep your hard-won lessons and most importantly… remember them, which were my "wins" in my Program. These passages were journal entries after meditation and mindfulness so I could remember my efforts and awakenings. Sometimes, as we get lonely and forget our pain-filled love adventures with our alcoholic, we can slip back (relapse) into nostalgia. It feels like falling asleep while completely awake. Program-people love to use a slang phrase called "our built-in forgetter." I was guilty of forgetting just how difficult loving an alcoholic can be.

My Lesson: Look to myself for the formula

I wrote this book to remember my mental math. I wrote this book to myself so that there would be no more living unconsciously and forgetting my reasons for leaving the alcoholic. I was done being pushed around by his alcoholism/-isms and by my fears. I wanted to remember my last brutal bottom that I experienced with this relationship, just as recovering alcoholics in AA try to remember their last drink to stick with sobriety.

Lessons learned + Lessons remembered
= Not repeating past mistakes

If you have already taken your life back, I urge you to keep it! May you stay awake and remember the craziness of being a player in an alcoholic relationship. May you remember the children who could/can/do get strung along, as well.

Before you get started:

If you are still involved with the alcoholic, admitting that you love an alcoholic is a significant first step. With self-honesty, you are then capable of establishing a policy of being lovingly truthful with yourself. Honesty and truthful living ultimately became my new clothes. You too can create your own personal contract with yourself, to live with truth.

If you are still stuck in the confusion stage, you can become willing to have the Truth revealed to you slowly as a good start. Willingness is another first step. As you become willing to deal with Reality, your mind can become open to the possibility of recovering cherished parts of yourself that you knew before this relationship. If you feel like you never had a self, you may begin to see that you can create yourself, birthing and building a new version of yourself in your lifetime. You can also begin to lift the veil of denial so that you may start to deal with the destruction of the disease. I call this ability "stopping the bleed." Always being mindful that I was in an alcoholic relationship helped stop the downward spiral into darkness. When I practiced toxic, codependent behaviors, pausing to name my situation is how I got a small amount of control over the loss and the drain of my power over to alcoholism. I consider it a significant step when I chose to stop the damage alcoholism had on my life. I believe this can occur at any point. The sooner, the better, of course!

Still suffering?

If you are still suffering, I believe that there is a miracle waiting for you on the other side of hitting your broken-hearted bottom. I equate "bottom hitting" to that of a spiritual awakening of sorts. It started my new math equation for a better life. I found my miracle to be a shift in my perception. Having the shift was a wonderfully empowering feeling that strengthened me on all levels and enabled me to take my power back. After all, how much more pain and suffering could I possibly endure?

I heard someone say that suffering was just another form of "processing" life. If that's the case, I had over-processed my alcoholic relationship. I bet you have endured some severe things as well and processed the heck out of the man. So, tell me... why would you keep choosing it? Can you find one stress-free reason?

It wasn't a mistake that I felt foreboding in my relationship with the alcoholic. It didn't take intelligence to foreshadow that there were storms of suffering available at every turn when loving an alcoholic man. There was ceaseless suffering in my mind, in my soul, and even real suffering in my physical body. It was a soul sickness I experienced with the alcoholic. Every act of betrayal, every lie, and every deception left me with violence in my soul.

I took a chance to break my codependency sickness and cut myself free before I actually "broke" or "cut" more of my life off from my dreams. At the time of ending the relationship with him, it felt like a real amputation. I had to cut off any ties to him as a way to save the rest of my person. It felt like a huge risk to try to live without the alcoholic. I had made him part of me. Separation was physically painful.

When this relationship turned its blackest of black, I became ready to learn my lessons. Are you ready to learn your lessons? Like, really learn them? Are you ready to stop repeating destructive patterns and forge a new path, take an exit, or embark down a different avenue?

It's a practice of good self-awareness to know...

◇ When do you lose yourself?
◇ Why do you lose yourself?
◇ How does this keep happening over and over? What's your pattern?

These are important questions that I asked myself, and I took the time to answer them.

Lesson: Ask yourself powerful questions

Throughout my inquiry into the alcoholic's chances of getting sober, I learned that logic, common sense, spirituality, community, and science play big roles in successful recovery from any form of addiction. It shocked me when someone in the Program told me that statistically an alcoholic man's chances of recovering from alcohol addiction was only 1%. They went further to say that ONLY those alcoholics that stayed in AA kept their sobriety. They ("The Winners") were the 1% of the 1 %. Those odds really stunned me. Were those slim-to-none odds true? The thought saddened me. I wanted my alcoholic to be one of the lucky ones. But reality and statistics were hard to ignore.

After hearing this data, not knowing if it was true, not able to find a reliable source of current statistics, I began to think about myself and my chances. Maybe talking numbers and creating math formulas for myself helped me give up the false hope I had? Maybe it was just what I needed to let him go. I thought to myself that if recovery in Alcoholics Anonymous was most likely his only hope of living happy, joyous, and free (some medical studies showed this to be the case), then I concluded that my recovery had to be my solution as well. I came to believe that my recovery was my best chance to live happy, joyous, and free. I wanted to stop waiting around hoping that he would leap into the 1% saved column so that I could finally be happy. I launched my "self-saving program" because I wanted to be the 1% saved (myself). I didn't have a drinking problem, but I had a relating in relationships problem.

I found The Al-Anon Family Groups to be a great program for me to attend regularly to learn more about the family disease of alcoholism, and most importantly, learn more about me. Twelve-Step support group rooms and long-time, faithful "recovery people" provided me enormous support for my enormous problem. Other fellow travelers who understood my situation (because they had lived it too) were the best aid in my healing process. They were the best listeners, and I needed someone to listen.

Today, there are many available avenues of healing and support. If it feels safe to do so, I encourage you to begin your healing process. You might start by looking for and attending support group meetings or private codependency addiction therapy. You might research codependency and love addiction and learn about these important topics from some several sources, like I did. I also found great explanations, and answers to some of my questions by researching alcoholism. Someone suggested to me that I learn all I could about the disease of alcoholism. So, I read the AA "big book" twice— even though I never identified as an alcoholic myself.

Lesson: Look to yourself for the formula

Do what feels right for you. Do what you feel ready for. Do what feels safe. Your steps are your steps as you explore recovering from the effects of the disease of alcoholism. I am always thrilled to see women shift from trying to save a toxic relationship with an active alcoholic to putting efforts into their own recovering and healing.

Once you feel safe, you may try taking some risks. You may take risks you are ready for. Taking risks repaired my broken relationship with myself.

I ask you...

✧ Can you repair the relationship with yourself?
✧ Can you recover yourself?
✧ Can you restore your lost energy and enthusiasm for living?
✧ Can you live the life your soul intended?

My answer to these questions was, "Yes! I can. And I will." So I did.

What's your math equation for a better life? Look to yourself for the formula.

So I'll ask you again... have you suffered enough?

"Merely consider and identify, while remembering that it is never too late for you to become the woman you were meant to be."
— Sarah Ban Breathnach, Simple Abundance:
A Daybook of Comfort and Joy

Stage I

The Very Codependent Caterpillar

Every End is a New Beginning

Crawling on the Ground Craving a Companion

(The end of lying to myself, the end of skepticism, and the end of a life without tools.)

...

"It's never too late to be what you might have been."
— *George Elliot*

*"Just when the caterpillar thought the world
was over, she became a butterfly."*
— *BARBARA HAINES HOWETT, Ladies of the Borobudur*

My First 3 Lessons

"Tell me, what is it you plan to do with
your one wild and precious life?"
— Mary Oliver, The Summer Day

Lesson #1

Admit the Truth

It's Okay to Love an Alcoholic

*"It's OKAY to be scared. Being scared means you're
about to do something really, really brave."*
— *Mandy Hale*

What is the truth?

10,000 hours, right? I had, what theorists say, the 10,000-hour
rule on the subject of loving an alcoholic. The principle says that
10,000 hours of "deliberate practice" are needed to become an
expert in any field (that's about 90 minutes per day for 20 years!).
If greatness requires enormous time, I certainly ought to have been
great at loving an alcoholic.

In 1999, after being in a relationship for three years, I finally felt
brave enough to attend an Al-Anon meeting for friends and family
of alcoholics. I attended at the suggestion of a therapist who was
listening to my woes and recounts of my boyfriend's drinking habits
and my concerns with it. I read a lot of the conference approved
literature, probably all of it, looking for answers for him. I went to
meetings for ten years only getting a little bit of relief for my anxiety

and still confused as to why I was there. At one Al-Anon meeting, on about the tenth year of attending, a pamphlet with the question "So you love an alcoholic?" printed on it, stopped me in my tracks. I took a deep breath and swallowed hard. I was loving an active alcoholic. (Yes, it took that long for me to see what was right in front of me.)

Silently, I struggled with this fact for a full ten years in the program, before I could ever speak up. I found this truth lodged in my heart. I sat in meetings with other women in a similar situation, yet I said nothing about my predicament. For ten years I just listened. I kept my own secrets, even secrets from myself. The word alcoholic was taboo to me. The word alcoholic had a stigma that I didn't want to associate myself with. My silence said that I believed it was not okay to love an alcoholic. I was silent because of my shame. The shame held me back from getting help. I had to admit what I was doing with my life if I could ever confront the issues. I discovered that I could only heal when I told the truth.

Lying to myself didn't heal me. I was warned about lying as a kid, but it was only explained to me that lying to others is what mattered. I didn't know I could lie to myself. As an adult, when I was seriously sick one year, a wise medically-intuitive woman warned me that liars don't heal. Ultimately, telling my truth set me free. It set me free to begin my healing process. I discovered that telling the truth to oneself is the start of the healing process. Admitting the truth set me free —to love who I loved and heal what needed healing.

My Lesson #1: Admitting the truth set me free

On the one hand, loving an alcoholic, felt like I was a child that was doing something wrong. For the first time in my life, love itself felt not okay. Wasn't the main theme of a fulfilling life supposed to be love? A part of me, the stuffed-in and shoved-down inner-self, was telling me that it was not okay to love this man. I had conflict. I felt like a tormented soul. I was scared loving an alcoholic. I was scared to tell the truth. I didn't want to admit this to anyone, myself included. How was I ever going to be able to stop loving him?

After my many, unsuccessful, yearly attempts to push this fact away, I came to realize that acceptance was the answer to my pain. I had to accept that I loved an alcoholic. I had to tell myself it was okay — it happened. It was okay to love an alcoholic (it felt true and I did). I began telling myself it was okay to love an alcoholic because I needed to hear some reassurance from my own heart and soul before I could move past this shock. I had to know that it was okay to love who I loved because I had been loving him for a long time.

When I admitted who I loved and that he was an alcoholic, shame welled up from within me each and every time because I was embarrassed by my choice of partner. My perfectionistic pride took a beating by being in the relationship. I know others saw the disrespect. Feeling like this love was a complete mistake triggered my fear of failure. What became irritating to my soul was watching myself continue to keep loving him over and over, and then loving myself less and less. I would stay in the relationship only to suffer more loss to alcoholism, hoping for gains. My soul recognized this and was silently suffering because I loved who I loved and didn't know how to change that. I felt humiliated by my life and my love.

I loved an alcoholic. After declaring this truth to myself, accepting this, understanding how it all happened, and choosing recovery, I came to believe that it was okay to love an alcoholic. After accepting myself and my choice of love partner, I ended my inner torment and stopped berating myself every time I confessed he was an active alcoholic. I needed to reassure myself that loving an alcoholic didn't make me bad, wrong, or stupid. However, loving him did have me feeling broken-hearted. This also pointed out that I had some problems with love. I began to not just study alcoholism, but also codependency.

Love or Fear?

Something about the concept of love shifted once I made peace with who I loved and what it meant. I had been loving an alcoholic for fifteen years of my life, and when I was suddenly alone, abandoned, and pregnant with his child, I realized my love was really fear. Realizing that my ongoing love was really fear spun my head around. I questioned myself... was what I felt so deeply for him just a private desperation and not really love at all? My brain couldn't comprehend love and fear being the same thing. Was my type of love (codependent love) really fear? What was love anyway?

This story of mine — about loving an alcoholic — is a journey that I choose to share. This is not a how-to instruction manual written to influence you in a way that would cause you to not love an alcoholic anymore. This is not a how-to guide to get over him. I am not suggesting that you stop loving him. I do suggest a change in you — of learning to love in different ways and learning to love yourself. I found that resisting the truth, the truth of loving him, only led to it persisting painfully. I found peace not by repressing my love but by transforming my love and expressing it through prayer. I achieved peace by curbing my compulsions and not giving in to urges of what I had been calling love.

I also changed my definition of love. I learned that having a new meaning for love and changing a definition (in my mind and heart) takes time. I struggled, as my beliefs took time to change, because I learned that my beliefs were the product of the thoughts that I kept thinking. I discovered that on the other side of changing beliefs was my transformation. Transformation took time. Time took time. I learned that for me, it took a long, long time and several lessons along the way.

Loving the alcoholic was so hard for so long. I began thinking that there might be something wrong with my concept of love in general. Loving an alcoholic, felt like a jail sentence. This love held me a prisoner. I wanted to believe that real love must be peaceful and not this chaos of alcoholism. After enough time in this painful relationship, I was willing to try out new kinds of love and give myself a chance for it. I decided to believe that real love must feel freeing and not anxiously depressing. So I needed to stop loving in the ways that caused me harm and heartache.

I looked at how I acted out my so-called love in my relationship. I looked at my so-called loving actions and realized I was enabling him. So I stopped. It was a start in the right direction when I looked at my actions of love that no longer served my new desire of becoming healthy, whole, and happy. I began to realize that my love (and "loving actions") may have been harmful to us both. I loved him in a hundred ways that did not work.

My next realization was that it's okay that I love an alcoholic, but I didn't have to...

live with him,

put up with him,

take him back,

allow him to treat me badly,

or listen to him.

I made a decision to stop with the alcoholic. I forced myself. I made a decision to wait, have patience, and seek a new kind of love. I adopted a type of love that let him go so that he was free to live the life he wanted to live. For so long, I was not okay with letting that happen. I was not okay with letting him go on his path the way he would choose. I was afraid. So who was the prisoner: me or him?

I discovered that by setting him free, I set myself free. I found this new freedom terrifying because it opened my life up to the unknown. I had many fears about not knowing things for certain.

I had to face various new forms of fear. However, with this freedom came different possibilities for my life, rather than the limitations that the unhealthy relationship held.

Still wondering... is this really love or is this fear?

It became important for me to begin to know that there was a difference between fearing and loving an alcoholic. Sometimes what I was calling love was really my fear portrayed as caretaking, saving, and rescuing to avoid pain and problems. Oftentimes, the ways I loved him was actually my fear of him and for him. I found myself professing my love ("but I love him so much!") to friends as an excuse to not fully let go. I believed that they couldn't understand my reasons for staying with him or going back. By saying I loved him, it was the same thing as saying, "I am so scared to lose him" or "I am afraid to be alone or confront the change it will bring in my life!" I had to start asking myself: is this really love or is this fear?

My fear of leaving the alcoholic was always tied with loving him. Another variation of fear that turned up in terms of loving an alcoholic is the fear that all my suffering and efforts were for nothing. I dreamed up jealousy that another woman would come in and take my place and receive all the happiness with this man that I worked so hard for (once he was cleaned up, in AA, and sober). Yet another variation was that I would miss out on our "happily-ever-after" together if I let him go to seek his version of "happily-ever-after" with alcohol. Fear of missing out was sometimes the biggest fear of all for me.

> *"People have a hard time letting go of their suffering. Out of a fear of the unknown, they prefer suffering that is familiar."*
> — *Thich Nhat Hanh*

However, I would hear other women's stories of a twenty-five-year marriage to alcoholism that would sober up this thought. Then I would wonder if I would just be missing out on more pain with the alcoholic. Truth was, I was holding on for dear life to this man and relationship out of fear. I had been betrayed and humiliated by this man's actions and behavior, but I continued to stand there even though I was ashamed just to be with him. That was my fear in freeze mode. Basically, when all my logic and good sense was gone, I felt pathetic because fear was keeping me in the relationship, not love.

Fearing my alcoholic was an important awareness. Fearing that he needed me in order for him to stay alive and be cared for, or fearing that I needed him to stay alive... was fear. Mothering a grown man, I concluded, is not love either. It certainly didn't feel like romantic love when I took the role of Mom for him. I found myself performing nurturing type of acts as if he were a small child, and it felt strange. I had crossed over into mothering and the relationship dynamic got mixed up. Fear was harmful to us both. I was afraid just as a mother would be for her son.

Loving him enough to let him go, on the other hand, was going to take a form of profound love. Trusting that he and I would be in a Higher Power's care when we parted paths was love. Trusting that it would work out in the highest and best for all concerned when I acted out of love and let him go instead of holding on for dear life was love.

When my new way of thinking about love set in and I began new actions of love, I was able to handle the fear with the use of love. I was able to face the loneliness, sadness, and grief that came when I disconnected from the tornado that is him and his life because it was out of love. I was able to think thoughts of hope, love, and compassion for us both because my reason was grounded in love. I was able to send a Christmas card with sincerity and not try to spend a Christmas with him in disappointment. Things changed for the better with each new practice of loving him yet being detached from his alcoholic world. I began practicing detachment with love.

When I confessed to my sponsor in recovery, "I don't think I loved him at all," my definition of love changed once again. My sponsor said, "we love with the capacity and definition of love at the time, and that changes." Hearing those words helped me release the shame of spending my love on an alcoholic. I loved the best way I could at the time. With the help of recovery, I learned to love the alcoholic but hate the progressive disease of alcoholism and what it had done to him. With even more time, I learned to love myself and stop fearing life. This is where I truly needed the 10,000 hours of experience!

So, I asked myself: "If I am this capable of loving an alcoholic so much, imagine how awesome I could be at loving myself?"

> *"Relationships are eternal. The 'separation' is another chapter in the relationship. Often, letting go of the old form of the relationship becomes a lesson in pure love much deeper than any would have learned had the couple stayed together."*
> — *Marianne Williamson*

Lesson #2

Seek Spiritual Solutions

Spiritual Power & Electricity

"Solutions can't be forced...
Spiritual solutions lead to serenity."
— *Excerpts from the suggested Al-Anon newcomer's welcome*

Is there a spiritual answer to alcoholism?

My sponsor, with over thirty years of recovery in The Twelve-Step Program of Al-Anon for friends and families of alcoholics, told me to listen closely and learn one vital thing if I wanted to recover from being affected by the disease of alcoholism. He told me, with complete assurance, that all the solutions to this complex problem were simple; he said, "all solutions are spiritual." I thought him a bold man to claim such a bold statement. Eleven years earlier, my first sponsor told me that all the tools of the program were like "power tools" and that in order for them to work, they had to be plugged into a power source (AKA a Higher Power) with a cord (AKA connection). That's when I came to learn about "spiritual electricity." Subscribing to spirituality was what accelerated my success and activated my recovery tools.

9

It was often suggested to me that I remember spiritual solutions, especially whenever I failed at forcing my will on the alcoholic. Some long-time program people told me that they considered alcoholism to be a spiritual disease thus requiring spiritual solutions. Some also believed that alcohol was just a symptom of a much deeper spiritual sickness. I didn't know what I believed. All I knew at the beginning of my recovery was that when I got sick from trying to solve this, when my life was unmanageable, that I had to go back to Step One of the program and admit powerlessness again. Then they suggested that I perform Step Two on my skeptical mind and come to believe in a Higher Power to restore me to sanity. The first three Steps of this Twelve-Step Program are about this all-powerful spiritual solution.

At my bottom, at my lowest point of loving an alcoholic, I was smart enough to suspend my disbelief of God and have an open-minded willingness. Even with my doubt, I concluded that there must be something helpful to the thousands of years of belief in a Higher Power. Others were sure that this was the best, most powerful, and most useful wisdom I could bless myself with, so I initiated myself to a Higher Power, without any church involvement. I began to pray. I discovered an important truth in loving an alcoholic: one of the most important things in life is my spiritual growth.

My Lesson #2: Some solutions are spiritual

When a wise woman in the program told me that nothing was more important than my spiritual growth, I was shocked by her claim. Weren't there a million more important things in life than an invisible walk with an invisible God, a Higher Power, or some type of spirituality? I needed real solutions! When I began trying to help myself through loving an alcoholic, I didn't even have a concept of God or a Higher Power. I had endless shelves of self-help books, and I was an avid reader on the subject. To me, self-help was credible, scientific, and had solutions, not some spiritual salve.

What I didn't know and what I didn't appreciate at the time was the tremendous power of spirituality. I didn't realize that it contained unseen forces against the darkness of the disease. I didn't understand that spiritual electricity existed. All I knew was that I had none and I never plugged into anything like it before. I relied on education, trying to convince myself that knowledge was the only power I needed. A god seemed far-fetched. If some solutions to the alcoholic situation were practical, I started to think some solutions may be spiritual.

When I acquired spirituality, I found that it was like being plugged into a power source just like my first sponsor said. I empowered myself with spiritual power. I could feel myself light up with each prayer prayed. At the start of my explorations in spirituality, I would believe in God for a while (when things were going well) and then "switch off" to disbelief when things were rough. When I felt like the God of my understanding had abandoned me, I recalled the famous "Footprints" poem, and leaned into imaginary loving arms. I understood that that's when a Higher Power was there for me in my footing and grieving. I came to know that spirituality served a purpose, and it wasn't for granting wishes. I needed spirituality when things were the hardest and no practical solutions worked. I came to rely on a Higher Power.

"He whispered, 'My precious child, I love you and will never leave you
Never, ever, during your trials and testings.
When you saw only one set of footprints,
It was then that I carried you.'"
— Margaret Fishback Powers, Footprints

After much searching, my sponsor's words finally meant something to me; the most important aspect to healing from the dilemma of loving an alcoholic is the evolution of my spiritual growth because I had to find a Loving Source of strength to carry me through this.

Spirituality offered new shifts to my stuck relationship state. I had spiritually synchronistic experiences I could not explain by

Earthly tangible forces. With what I call "spiritual sight" I would see things that would show up for me (right on time) when I needed them most. I began to see spirituality grow within someone... me! Perhaps, that's when I truly began to see life in all its mystery. I discovered serenity to be sacred and sourced from a Higher Power. I found all the sustainable solutions to the problem of loving an alcoholic to indeed be spiritual. I survived on spirituality. As I saw it, I had two choices: I could believe in a beneficial Higher Power or not believe. Those were my choices, and I chose to believe.

Through my prayers, I saw spiritual solutions arrive. Sometimes these were basic, like when I prayed for my portion of daily bread when the alcoholic shunned responsibility of me and our child and we had no money for food. Spiritual solutions began arriving when I got spiritual. Having spiritual electricity empowered me to speak up and set things straight.

As I recovered, learned, and healed with spirituality I was able to cultivate some serenity within myself and home. When I was not able to contain the pain, I rested in the invisible loving arms of a Higher Power to get me through my every fear (and every tear). What makes my version of a Higher Power so incredible and so high-powered is that my Higher Power was untouched by the disease of alcoholism. I found a source of strength that wasn't a drinking, depressed, alcoholic man and that made all the difference! I declared for myself that the alcoholic was no longer my Higher Power!

When I stopped thinking that I knew what was best for the alcoholic, things changed for me. I stopped thinking I was the best thing for him. I stopped trying to be his God, Higher Power, and savior. Instead, I sought my own higher source. I sought spirituality. I stopped thinking the drinker belonged with me or to me. I stopped casting self-help spells over him with my selfishness, hoping that he would change and smarten up so I could have him all to myself so I could be happy.

There is a funny saying about life that really pulls me back to reality, "no one gets out of here alive." With a current average expected lifespan of approximately eighty years, I had to look at what I wanted to do with that time. With my first thirty years, I chose to actively love an active alcoholic. That path led me through humiliating and extreme pain, as well as facing many problems. Ultimately, I had to face myself as my biggest problem of all. I had to ask myself, "what did I want to do with my final fifty years?"

By finding a Higher Power of my own, I felt the relief of being separate from the alcoholic and alcoholism. I stopped being so enmeshed with him and his disease. I became my own person with power. I started to realize we are all special souls, free to be on our own very personal journey. It finally occurred to me that that included the alcoholic. He was a man who had that right to freedom, too. He, as an active alcoholic, even had the right to fail. I've heard it said that we each have a path we must follow, and so I finally let him follow his, for then I was free to follow mine.

Thankfully, my path led me to the Program of Al-Anon. I started to walk a path of spiritual growth, practicality, and maturity. The tough lessons felt like an uphill climb at times, but I found that on the other side of those mountains were refreshing air-filled awakenings and brilliant awarenesses. Whilst in the relationship with the alcoholic, the continual pain of the dilemma kept me in a close walk with a Higher Power. Pain brought me to the feet of a Higher Power. I started my spiritual practices of channeling my pain into prayers, I prayed out loud for five minutes a night on my knees and spent ten minutes each morning in silence with a Higher Power. I stayed inspired through study, worship music, and talking to other believers. My spiritual life began. These were my "Spiritual Exercises."

I now believe that one of my most important walks in life is my walk with a Higher Power of my understanding. Spiritual growth and maturity saved me. I learned how important my connection to a loving, helpful Higher Power was to my survival. Unplugging from the alcoholic's energy source and using a Higher Power to generate love in my life was the lesson.

Loving an alcoholic was a choice I made. It may have been an unconscious, automatic choice in the past, but today I recognize it was still a choice. I wasn't a prisoner of love, even though I felt imprisoned. When I came to see that the jailor was me and when I came to believe in a Higher Power, I found the key. I unlocked myself from these chains of the crisis because the alcoholic never was going to do it for me. So why had I handed him the key, asking for his sobriety?

That awareness of having choices about everything in my life launched an awakening. It called me to battle for my life and for me to bail myself out. That choice strengthened my ability to advocate for myself. As I learned to sail the rough waters with my survival ship, I gained better navigation skills. I learned to navigate changes and choices.

"I am not afraid of storms, for I am learning how to sail my ship."
— *Louisa May Alcott, Little Women*

If I was making unconscious choices my whole life before I became conscious of those choices, and if life was all about learning lessons, I often questioned whether loving an alcoholic was my best choice of path to take. When I doubted myself in this way, my sponsor assured me that I would have eventually had to learn these lessons at some point in my life. I had to agree that the journey in this direction was my greatest opportunity for learning and spiritual growth because there was always a problem I was up against with him or within myself. I was building "spiritual muscles" by having to lift all the heavy problems of facing alcoholism and battling codependency. Because I broke and was broken hearted, I was able to break through my skepticism in a Higher Power. From that place, I welcomed my spiritual growing power. I chose to plug into the "spiritual grid." And I asked myself this question, "how can spirituality save me?"

"For we walk by faith, not by sight."
— *2 Corinthians 5:7*

Lesson #3

Work Recovery

My Recovery

"If one person gets into recovery, the whole family benefits."
— an Al-Anon saying

I wondered... if my love couldn't save him, could my recovery save him?

My recovery didn't save him. I repeat: my recovery didn't save my alcoholic. My solo, personal recovery didn't save our relationship. It didn't heal him, it didn't fix him, and it didn't spare him the problems or pain of his own making, no matter how often I prayed it would. I realized that I couldn't give my recovery away to anyone. I worked my own Twelve Step Recovery Program in Al-Anon, went to meetings, prayed, and begged my Higher Power for divine interventions for him, but in the end, my recovery didn't fix his drinking problem.

What I came to learn was that my recovery, while not effective in changing him like I originally wanted, did fix parts of my life. My recovery healed me, shaped me, and spared me from more problems and pain in the alcoholic situation. My recovery did save me.

My Lesson #3: My recovery is for me, work my recovery

My recovery saved me from continuing a long, tiring journey of behaving like a needy, soulless, toxic, and enabling codependent for the rest of my life. Even more so, for a nine-month period of my life, my recovery saved my unborn baby from a miscarriage, because I was courageous enough to cut ties and communication with the alcoholic as an effort to lower my stress. As a result of my recovery, my baby survived. My recovery was about my recovery from the effects of the disease of alcoholism. In truth, I had been severely affected.

Would working recovery be worth it?

My recovery became my own version of what it takes to recover. My recovery was my own blend of the Twelve-Step Program of Al-Anon for friends and family of alcoholics mixed with other various self-help resources. When I thought about hard work, I envisioned blood, sweat, and tears. And that's just what it took. I added some private counseling from a local domestic violence agency for women and a good amount of mentoring from several spiritual directors. Hard work is usually defined as requiring a great deal of effort and endurance. I went to work and attended 90 meetings in 90 days for my baby when I discovered I was pregnant. Then I went to 90 more just for me, as her mom. We both needed the meetings. Making those meetings took tremendous effort and placed me in the hands and heart of the program.

It is a wonderful thing to look back and see how every decision I made with program principals, good motives, and clear intentions (such as reducing my stress while pregnant) ultimately saved my baby from gestational harm, complications, and potential life-long problems that we now know maternal stress can do to a fetus. Certainly, my recovery spared me more heartbreak. Most importantly, it spared my child and me from living in an alcoholic home.

As my beautiful baby girl grew up, I grew up too, "working my program." I began to witness and see a bigger, fuller picture of what my new healthy recovery behaviors did for us both. Living my recovery prevented more harm, stress, and problems for us. Big decisions that I made, which took massive amounts of courage, helped her survive and thrive. In trying moments of uncertainty, I pushed through by asking for help from my Higher Power, from people I felt safe with, and from people who I could depend on. Asking for help in the right places and from the right people paid off. I learned the alcoholic couldn't help me, and I finally learned to stop asking.

Helping myself and taking more responsibility was what mattered. It eliminated our vulnerabilities to the alcoholic and alcoholism. Most of my toughest efforts required inner battles that I had to conquer on the inner fronts. I had to let go and tackle (with my recovery) my ridiculous pride, my sneaky self-shame, my ongoing self-doubt and my ingrained guilt. Facing those feelings became my personal wins and changed me. My personality changes sent my child and mine's life in a very different direction. The new path I forged had to be laid out by me, brick by brick, tear by tear, atop of fear after new fear. I believe that the recovery path led us to greener pastures and better outcomes.

I have often wished my recovery could have saved others whom I loved and cared for and were suffering from this disease. I had to learn that my recovery was mine, and meant for me alone. Even after leaving the alcoholic relationship, I wished my recovery could influence my child's father for her sake. I wanted the miracles of recovery for everyone. After failed attempts at trying to make miracles happen (with my will and on my timeline), I now know that it was my miracle for me, and just me, and just in time! I could only share the power of my story with whoever was willing to listen and whoever was open to my message of triumph over tragedy.

Recovery "rub-off"

To my relief and delight, my recovery rubbed off on my child every day that I stayed sane and serene. As a fetus in my womb, a newborn, a baby, a toddler, and then a little blond curly-haired girl, her little heart was willing and open to receive all the goodness, love, freedom, joy, and happiness that my recovery had to offer. I am grateful that she was privileged by my recovery. She witnessed better days than what could have been had I stayed with her father. She avoided those discouraging days of confusion, conflict, sadness, sorrow, despair, and depression that come with active alcoholism. Escaping that lifestyle of hell (of living with an active alcoholic) was just one of the steps I took. I also had to confront my codependency (which was originally termed Co-Alcoholism) because I was prone to obsessive focus and anger with the alcoholic — even out of the relationship! I had to work on myself or risk her being neglected by my compulsive alcoholic focus, which was festering inside me and always leading me emotionally down into despair and rage. I had to be brutally honest about my reasons for the many times I relapsed into my codependent side of the sickness.

Because of my recovery and my commitment to sticking with the Program, my daughter, a child of an alcoholic, was able to and has been able to experience the best version of me as a mother: a version of me who was peaceful in the morning, waking up in my own energy, and walking in my power. With recovery, I was finally available to myself, available to life, and available to my child.

By just being free in my own home, I cried many tears of freedom. I remember during the first few years after I ended the relationship, I would cry in the mornings. I was surprised that I could cry so many tears of relief from being able to escape the grip of anxiety of being in that type of relationship. My mornings became sun-filled, quiet, and serene. I couldn't remember having those experiences since I was a carefree little girl myself. I felt so grateful for not choosing to remain in his endless depressions and sufferings whilst falsely thinking I could help him (or falsely thinking it was my job to help him). Free of an alcoholic relationship, I felt the wonder of how wonderful the early, quiet hours were before the day began. I could hear the birds chirping and realized they were actually singing!

With the choice to end an alcoholic relationship and enough practice of recovery principles, I could appreciate and be present to a beautiful sunrise and not awaken to a moaning, miserable, unhappy active alcoholic man with endless criticisms and complaints. I finally felt free! What I want to tell you is… my recovery didn't save him, but it did save me! I wasn't afraid of hard work since it had led to my freedom. Where else in my life did I need to do some work?

"Recovery, first it gets better,
Then it gets worse,
Then it gets Real,
Then it gets real different!"
— Anonymous

The Road is Which Way?

Strangled by self-doubt,
Suffering subtle self-loathing,
Suffocating in a swamp of self-pity,
Staring straight backwards,
Shaming for senseless past mistakes,
Stuck, frozen, unable to move,

Too long of a pause,
Too much of a stop,
Too deep a standstill,
Too sidetracked,
Too distracted,

I forced myself to face forward again.
I asked, "The road is which way?"

— Grace Wroldson

Lesson #4

Don't Lie

The BIG Lie

"The only thing you need to change is everything."
— An AA Sponsor announced

Who was lying?

I lied when I spoke the "truth" to myself. The BIG lie I told myself as a codependent woman with a serious love addiction who was infatuated with an alcoholic man was, "if he just quits drinking... everything would be okay." That recurring thought was part of my denial. It was what I had hoped. That was the part of me that was immature, naive, and ignorant. That was the part of me not fully understanding the disease of alcoholism and addiction. That was the part of me that did not take the disease seriously.

"There are two ways to be fooled. One is to believe what isn't true; the other is to refuse to believe what is true."
— Søren Kierkegaard

If he was not getting better, how were things going to get better for our relationship? How was recovery supposed to help save our relationship if I was the only one in recovery? I would momentarily forget about the "-isms" of alcoholism, also known as the character flaws and habits that made my life so miserable with this man. The truth was that there were other issues preventing my happiness with him than just his drinking. I attended several open AA meetings and learned that when, and if, an alcoholic gets into recovery, he then faces the challenges of completely changing himself. This included, with the help of his sponsor, fixing his broken moral compass.

> *"You can fool yourself, you know. You'd think it's*
> *impossible, but it turns out it's the easiest thing of all."*
> — *Jodi Picoult, Vanishing Acts*

I failed to understand that the disease of alcoholism had many aspects. Alcoholism is often called a threefold disease of the mind, body, and spirit. There were physical, mental, emotional, and spiritual problems brewing in us both. I witnessed all aspects of alcoholism, and his life was affected. Our relationship was affected. I was being affected by the disease by being around him and, especially, by being attached to him. I woke up one day and realized that if I was going to be so easily influenced, then I want to be influenced positively by recovery.

My Lesson #4: Don't lie to myself

I wanted to get the truth straight into my head and stop lying to myself. I started asking myself simple but straightforward, probing questions like:

- ✧ Does his drinking bother me?
- ✧ Is he a positive person to be around or is he always in a negative frame of mind?
- ✧ Does he have a way of communicating that leaves me feeling confused and awful?

✧ Is he in good health?

✧ Are his finances a mess or always a big problem for him?

✧ Does he do self-work and get help for the problems he has in his life?

✧ Is he an inspiration to me?

✧ Does he rely on a Higher Power or just drink more when life gets tough?

✧ Do I respect him?

This quick inventory of questions about his alcoholism made me realize that getting him to simply put down a drink would not slay the monsters I was battling in our relationship. I took truthful stock and found that all aspects of him were being affected by this disease called alcoholism. His thoughts were negative, fear-based, old, stale, and stuck. His physical body was not being taken care of or "kept-up." His emotions were up and down, and he never experienced contentment or serenity— ever. His connection to a Higher Power was non-existent. There was nothing higher than his overinflated ego. He could not hear God (Good Orderly Direction) over the critical voice in his head and his parents' past remarks. The pressures of his past haunted him and, seemingly, chased him to the next drink. I knew he felt empty, like a lost boy most of the time.

I asked myself, did I really want to share a life with these issues? Because as out of touch with reality as I was, I knew, if I based my life on him, I would be signing up for all of him – all of this. A thought that occurred to me was that major work had to be done on his personality for him to be healthy enough to be in a healthy relationship with anyone! He would need to undergo a complete personality change to be the happy and fulfilled man that I could enjoy life with.

The alcoholic would need more than sobriety to participate in a good life with me. He would need that sparkle in his eye and be truly happy with his life to make a great partner. He would have to bring his personal happiness to the relationship to have a happy relationship. Despite what the alcoholic thought, happiness was not a "plate" served up by a happy woman. I realized that lasting happiness would require that he, also, be happy and bring happiness to the table.

That was what stuck out the most for me. The alcoholic was clearly not happy, and drinking was as close as he could get to feeling good. From where I sat at this table, to reach his version of inner happiness and contentment with life would require significant changes. These changes would then have to be not only established but also, sustained, which is an incredibly difficult task. I came to think that this would take more than the support from others, tools, and an AA program. The task was boundless; it required him to grow out of his old thinking habits and develop completely new thought processes. It was beyond just stopping drinking or quitting alcohol. It would take a whole lot of work in recovery to change the entire script of his life and the repeated patterns of his subconscious. Wait!? Am I talking about myself or the alcoholic?

> *"An alcoholic is not cured just because they stopped drinking.*
> *Remember, "the drinking" for the alcoholic is only a*
> *symptom of an underlying problem within him or her. Total*
> *sobriety takes more than abstinence--it takes a spiritual*
> *and mental awareness through healing and growth."*
> — *Angie Lewis, The Alcoholism Trap*

My recovering alcoholic grandfather reminded me that this was a family disease. The traits, the limited beliefs, the habits, the compulsions, the unhealthy solutions, the fears, and the bad vocabulary are passed down through the family, and the alcoholic I loved was a culmination of that, too, just like I was. However, I was taught to be a codependent caretaker, and my disease took on another form. Was I happy?

Finally, I came to the conclusion that he was not my job. I was my job. So, my first task was to stop lying to myself. My job was to face reality and own up to the BIG lie I was telling myself. My job was to get clear about who he really was and let go of the man I fantasized he could be. My job was to examine and remember his behavior, not his words. My job was to realize reality. My job was to understand that there was more to this problem of loving an alcoholic. My job was to stop blaming "the drink." I checked in with my own moral compass, and I asked myself, "was I going to continue to lie to myself?"

"Don't be sorry for the truth. A harsh truth is less damaging than a tender lie, and the worst lies are the ones we tell ourselves."
— *Dianna Hardy, The Spell of Summer*

Lesson #5

Use Common Sense and Logic

Common-Sense Crisis

"One day you finally knew
what you had to do, and began,
though the voices around you
kept shouting
their bad advice--...
But you didn't stop.
You knew what you had to do..."
— Mary Oliver, The Journey

It wasn't so much a relationship crisis, rather, I had a complete common-sense crisis. I crashed. I was dating the same man over and over but expecting a different relationship. Where was the common sense in that?

com·mon sense defined:
good sense and sound judgment in practical matters

A part of me knew it was a high-risk game of love to be involved with an alcoholic. One definition of insanity is doing the same thing over and over yet expecting a different result! I knew it was insane to keep being in this on-and-off relationship with him, breaking up, and later taking him back. The relationship felt emotionally super-charged; my feelings were always heightened, and my emotions were on high alert. I knew it was unreasonable for me to give the relationship another chance or the "one more try" each time after he had strayed and came back. I lost count of how many rounds of relationships I did with this same man. Simply the fact that the pain-filled relationship needed another chance, and the fact that our relationship had been broken before, was a red flag. Why could I not see those red flags telling me that something was wrong? If this love wasn't a game, it certainly was a bumpy road! With the internal drugstore of adrenaline, cortisol, and hormones flowing, my mind wasn't clear enough to see this relationship's road nor the many stop signs. Even if the red flags weren't enough to stop me then why didn't I stop at the obvious bright red blinking stop signs with this man?

Upon entering my recovery in the Twelve Step Program of Al-Anon, I faced my personal common-sense crisis. I was running my life, rather ruining my life by, using very little common sense. My decisions were emotions-based; I was following my heart, or so I thought. I believed following my heart was a way to a painless life with unending happiness. I wanted to get it "right" this next time with him. With each relationship failure, I had to face my pain and utter disappointment. After the flood of tears stopped, and my genuine grieving was underway, I realized that I was falsely following my impulses, urges, and compulsions. My investment in him was irrational and illogical. I was driven by my fears, anxieties, and abandonment issues, not by my heart. I ended up bankrupt and broke of not just self-love, but logic as well.

The codependent spell

When I "woke-up" from the codependent spell, I asked myself, "what happened to my common sense?" I thought I had it once, before I had entered the romantic relationship with an alcoholic. Where did it go? Wait, where did I go?

My Lesson #5: I must use common sense and logic

Whenever I looked at my decimated life through the clear lens of common sense, I felt ashamed and embarrassed. In recovery, I was working hard to see more clearly at every turn and learn how to slow down at every yellow blinking warning light. My problem was that I was emotionally speeding and going 100 miles per hour through life. No wonder I didn't see the stop signs with the alcoholic. I was fleeing from painful feelings rather than facing them. When I took the time to stop and learn about codependency, I found myself spelled out. I learned that codependents turn on themselves, and I found that to be the scariest symptom of my sickness. How could I protect myself if I often turned on myself? This was an unnatural, unhealthy characteristic that went against self-preservation and towards a subtle, strange, self-inflicted death. My codependency was slow suicide.

Anytime I was in the relationship with the alcoholic, I lost myself in that relationship. I allowed myself to be consumed by painful romance. To be with him, I wore my dark sunglasses of denial and drove on his road. I had to use a complex justification system to stay in his truck and on the road of his life. I had to tell stories to myself to convince myself to stay, and I had to tell bigger stories to my friends to explain why. I deceived myself by only focusing on what I wanted to see when the relationship was "good." In hindsight, I've realized that I only saw what I could see at the time. Anything that made me feel uneasy, I sugar-coated with an odd love language, or I looked the other way. It was my way to cope and to "keep" him. I did not have the awareness of myself in relationships, and I had very few relationship tools to work with. Ignoring and skipping over disturbing things was how I made it so many years. That was my denial in action. Denial had protected me from the pain of my reality.

Denial and distorted thinking

Along with the alcoholic's continual drinking, there was a progression in my distorted thinking. Mental deterioration left me with an inability to sort out my thoughts. I became confused. Then, sorting out my feelings became a struggle, too. Basically, my common sense "went out the window" because I did not like what I saw nor was involved in. The truth was too painful to pay any attention to. Without knowing it, I had to keep up with the crazy chaos. In order to hang on, I had to apply a thick coat of "didn't-see-that-denial" to my life in order feel uncomfortably okay about our relationship.

Towards my bottom, I began thinking from a very skewed place which really did not make any sense at all. Sadly, this backwards thinking supported my decision to stay in the relationship. I was determined and desperate to hang onto my fantasy with him. I settled for extracting fleeting moments of pleasure from an awful and disrespectful relationship.

Over the years of dating this man, there were a few important facts that my denial could not contain nor conceal. One fact was that drinking is itself an unconscious behavior. When he was drinking, he checked out. Conversely, and ironically, I was personally working hard to be on a conscious path in life. I was educated, practicing yoga and meditation, and immersed in self-help knowledge. I knew that a drinking person (someone who is intoxicated) goes out of their regular mind and into an altered state. Why did knowing that not help me? That's when it dawned on me that I was trying to be with someone who was not actually "there." As his disease progressed, I noticed that he preferred the altered state. Right before I ended the fifteen-year-old relationship, I realized that he needed to be intoxicated to enjoy my company. That observation made me feel sad and, mostly, it was about myself.

Unfortunately, not knowing any better at the time, I mistakenly took his unhappiness personally. I felt like I was not good enough. I did not feel special or exciting enough. I felt like I was not interesting enough to keep my man entertained and happy. I mistakenly thought that his discontentment with his life was my fault. Sometimes, I even, pressured myself, thinking maybe I just needed to be a sexier woman!

What is normal?

I understood that common sense could not exist with an unconscious existence being the norm. There was always chaos and a mess to clean up or step over. Drinking was his norm. Consequently, in order for me to stay in relationship to this depressed drinking man, denial became my norm. This was how I became crazy and was in a common-sense crisis of my own. My common sense seriously diminished to the point where nothing made sense in my life, nor his! I was working a job that I hated, living in a place I was embarrassed about, befriending other sick people – mistakenly thinking that they were loving and kind souls who knew my pain of loving him and understood my reasons for taking him back. Those sick friends blessed my relationship with the alcoholic, so I kept them. I kept my enablers.

I had as many excuses as there are words to hold on to my relationship to the alcoholic. I often whined to family and friends, "but I love him, and love does not always make sense." Thankfully, with the help of Al-Anon friends who practiced recovery, I ultimately chose not to live by that saying. I saw it for what it was: justification for living an unhappy, confused life! In recovery, I learned another saying, one that was true, "sometimes love just ain't enough!" I regained my common sense and realized that my love couldn't stop his alcoholism. I had living proof. I began to truly understand that alcoholism was a disease. I learned that alcoholism affects the whole family system and anyone else it touches. I was touched.

Near my bottom, the obviousness of my problems still did not shake me out of my denial. My life started to be utterly destroyed by his disease. Coming to awareness was painful, but living my life became worse. The reality was hard to swallow and stomach. I, cynically, blocked my own tears with buried rage as a flood precaution. I was smart, educated, competent, and yet, I still was unable to make a healthy choice in love. Something was wrong with me, I decided. It could not be all the alcoholic's fault. I played a part in this so-called life of mine. My fears played a bigger part. I was afraid to be embarrassed by another failure. I was angry with myself. I was hurt. I didn't want to grieve the relationship. I was afraid of the pain that would overcome me; I was afraid to be swallowed by my sorrow. I was too emotionally sick to let go and leave.

Fear

Fear was my enemy. Fear distorted my thinking every time I wanted to break up and leave. I declined into a warped excuse system, where I compromised myself. I reverted to immature teenage love thinking and went toward my fantasy-thinking, denying that the relationship was really that bad. Following fearful thinking, and acting on these thoughts, is what led me to a life that made no sense; a life from which I then suffered. It took me years to admit that I did not have to be the drinker to end up in Messed-Up Ville (a fictional place my life often went every time I was involved with him). I became aware that all I had to do was spend my life with an unconscious drinker and for the disease to rub off on me. I became the second victim of the disease of alcoholism. I became insane. I lost the ability to function with common sense. As a result, I got seriously and severely sick myself with co-alcoholism (codependency).

There came a time when I was actually bed-bound with the codependency sickness that I asked myself, "did I really want to be the second victim of the disease of alcoholism?" I wasn't even the one who was drinking! Was I okay with this happening to me? Or shall I say, was I okay with allowing this ugly progression to continue in my life?

Thankfully, I knew that I could only control what was going to happen in my life, to an extent. Controlling him and his life was off the table of things I could or should manage. It only followed logically that if I was engaging with, talking to, or spending time with an active drinker, I was stepping into a realm where distorted thinking and crazy-making conversations would breed more toxic thought patterns. With distortion in my mind and life, common sense had NO bearing on reality. No wonder my life was so unmanageable! I was not grounded in logic; I was not centered in common sense, and this was my biggest problem.

Myself first

With serious mental effort and many millions of reminders, I began to start to think about myself first. I learned one definition of codependency to be, a normal reaction to an abnormal person. What that definition lacked was the follow up of "and then you become abnormal, by always reacting!" I needed friends to remind me every day that my thoughts had wandered back to the alcoholic and away from myself. For months after ending the alcoholic relationship, including ending all communication with him, I heard reruns of his sayings, lectures, and words in my head that I needed to empty and purge.

"You plant corn, you get corn," my alcoholic would say to me whenever I faced failure. This was something he heard from his old farmer father. This was something I heard and understood with a sad certainty. With my new awareness and growing strength, I knew this saying applied in a way he (the alcoholic) would not enjoy hearing. I no longer wanted to plant disease and get more disease. I no longer wanted to water this disease waiting for it to sprout further into our lives. I was willing to change, grow, and plant my garden elsewhere. I wanted to be somewhere, and with someone, where my happiness stood a real chance of growing into my dreams. To me, his family's saying was about making sense in life and planting elsewhere finally made sense. I wanted a life that made sense. I was planting my dreams, and I knew I would get them. (You plant your dreams, you get your dreams.)

Crafting common sense and getting me back

Determined to get myself back, and to stay focused on myself, I made some vows to myself. I proclaimed that it was time to get back to using my common sense! I declared that it was time for me to face reality. I vowed to begin using logic again and actually apply it to my life – not just think it. There came a day when I spoke out loud to myself, "I will not self-sabotage. I will self-protect!"

I heard a man say over and over in the rooms of Al-Anon, "if you always do what you have always done, then you will always get what you always got." Well, I did not like what I was getting. I wanted something better. Common sense said that my "something better" could not come from him nor being with him. I learned that a better life had to come from me. I needed a logical version of me to create a happy life for myself.

Personally, I needed a good dose of Common Sense 101. I tried hard to bring my thinking back to making some sense. There came a day when I was finally no longer afraid to admit a common-sense truth to myself. The truth was: I could not be in a healthy relationship with an unhealthy man. Common sense said this truth to me: I was not that powerful to control the thoughts, feelings, reactions, triggers, and wills of two people. I barely had control over my own will. The alcoholic never asked me to run his life nor fix him. I learned firsthand that if I tried to make someone sick become healthy, I would get sick, too. Controlling was sick and exhausting behavior.

I badly needed the linear language of logic. I experienced very little confusion with things that had common sense, like paying my bills on time. I had to face what common sense dictated in my situation with an alcoholic. Facing common sense and true logic dictated making different life choices. It meant making a totally different relationship choice. Before I could ever make different choices and sustain them, it meant thinking differently. First of all, it meant slowly coming out of my denial and getting dagger-distance away from my crisis. I learned that if it doesn't make sense: it doesn't make sense. So, now, if it doesn't make sense, then I stop trying to make sense of it.

Once I was being truthful and honest with myself, everything started to make sense. I was loving an alcoholic, but not loving myself. My primary problem was the lack of self-love. This was the root of all my other problems in my life.

Then, I created my own personal Common Sense 101 Self-Study Course; it began like this:

- ✧ Common sense is not… worrying and anticipating the worst, while choosing to remain in an unhealthy relationship that consistently gives me obvious reasons to worry and anticipate bad things.
- ✧ Common sense is not… dating, being intimate with, getting engaged to, marrying, nor being close friends with an unhealthy man with a drinking problem.
- ✧ Common sense is not… taking an ex (who stills drinks) back. An ex is an ex for a reason!
- ✧ Common sense is not… trying to spend time and get attention from an emotionally unavailable and immature man.

⬦ Common sense is not...trying to fix a man when he is not willing and does not want to truly change. (Note to self: If he did want to change and if he was willing, he would have already changed FOR HIMSELF, not me!)

⬦ Common sense is not... witnessing a man be cruel, inconsiderate, neglectful, cold, uncaring, critical, or unkind to another person (this includes his mother) and thinking that I am the exception and that he would never do that to me.

⬦ Common sense is not... doing things for a grown man that he should be doing for himself. (This includes doing his adult thinking for him.)

⬦ Common sense is not... living my life solely for the purpose of being in a romantic relationship. There is way more to life.

⬦ Common sense is not... trying to make something feel OKAY, that doesn't feel OKAY. (Note to self: I need to listen and respect my gut feelings.)

⬦ Common sense is not...contorting myself to try to make something feel right, that doesn't feel right.

⬦ Common sense is not... hoping something that doesn't make sense now will make sense later.

Common sense was clearly not these things. This was the contrast I needed to see and come to know. I established this list for myself as a reminder and a tool for clarity. It was a self-study course I needed to take over and over. My life wasn't working with the alcoholic. Furthermore, my life wasn't working being, me. I confess that I had a common-sense crisis. However, I knew there was an opportunity here for me. What was my opportunity?

"In the Chinese language, the word "crisis" is composed of two characters, one representing danger and the other, opportunity."
— *John F. Kennedy*

Lesson #6

Stop Asking Why

My Curious Case of the "Whys"
(Diagnosing and Self-Treating My Case of the "Whys")

I wondered why?

- ✦ Why didn't my relationship work?
- ✦ Why me? Why did I have to love an alcoholic, anyway?
- ✦ Why did he do that to me!?
- ✦ Why can't he be here for me in the way I need him?
- ✦ Why did this betrayal happen to me?
- ✦ Why can't I have a happy life with him?
- ✦ Why does another woman get to have him?
- ✦ Why should I have to do this program called recovery, be single, and alone?
- ✦ Why can't things be easier for me?

When my fantasies and outer-happiness didn't pan out in loving an alcoholic, I found myself constantly asking "why." This questioning behavior was my pure self-doubt sickness. It was like having a fever of self-pity; I liken it to having a common cold virus, and I called it coming down with a case of the "whys."

Having the "whys" kept me stuck in a victim mentality. I was like a wailing and whining two-year-old who didn't get her candy. Continuously asking "why" was my biggest stumbling block to moving forward. What was worse was that I had a case of the "poor me's" to go with it.

I knew that not all questions that start with "why" were bad questions to ask. However, I witnessed myself using this question to avoid facing reality and to avoid being in the here-and-now. I was using this word as a weapon with friends and my Higher Power. It became self-detrimental, as it carried on without an end. I was stalling my growth by stopping and always asking why.

Lesson #6: Stop myself from asking why

My "whys" were a symptom of being affected by the disease of alcoholism. My "whys" were a major part of my codependency issue. Constant questioning showed my inability to let go. The constant questioning of reality highlighted my suffering and definitely added to it. Anyone clearly listening to me at the time could tell I was unwilling to let go of the alcoholic— unless someone gave me a good answer to my whys!

What was wrong with the simple answer of "no one knows" and being okay with that? I used questioning as a way to not grieve the end of the relationship. I used it to avoid facing my losses. Practicing and reciting the "whys" only spun me around in a circle. I was unable to make progress in my recovery by continually asking "why?" Maybe, I subconsciously knew that others in recovery didn't have all the exact answers to my situation, so I found a way to passively attack the Program and discredit it. After all, according to the Big Book of Alcoholics Anonymous, alcoholism is baffling, cunning, and powerful – maybe, I fell right into its trap?

I had my motives. One motive for my repeated asking was because I thought if I knew the answer I could then possibly fix things. However, my newer, healthier self-recovery mission was to get out of my "fix-it" mentality. Ironically, I was trying to fix that, too!

I had done enough years of loving an alcoholic to know that "fixing him" always seemed to be at my expense: financially, physically, mentally, emotionally, and spiritually. Plus, my Band-Aids never truly worked on a gaping wound that needed a Higher Power's stitching. It was more than I could humanly accomplish. After looking at our wounded relationship, I realized it was worse each time. That is when I understood that, when it came to him, I had to remove "why" from my vocabulary. Asking "why" would be allowed if it was to question my motives and behavior. I had to take a look at where I was asking this question in a useful manner. That included angrily crying, "why God?!" Before "working the Program," I was a victim, or so I thought.

What I knew was that there was a good chance that I might never get truthful, real answers to my questions of why. Even more so, I knew I may never get that one satisfying answer to quench my thirst for understanding the alcoholic. Thus, I was forced to breathe in the uncertainty and unknowingness of life, and learn to sit uncomfortably there. And, it surely was uncomfortable!

Could I be okay without ever getting an answer? I had to be. I could no longer spend my life waiting and "whying" for answers that no one could give me, especially not the confused and lost alcoholic. When I began incessantly asking "why?", I was, truth be told, complaining. When I was in this "undercover" complaint mode, I couldn't get anywhere farther in life but where I was.

One day, after having this curious case of the Whys for around ten years, I finally had had enough of myself! I was tired of being plagued by my victim mentality. I learned that it was self-responsibility to quit asking. Complaining kept me negative, and I was exhausted with complaining. Complaining was what I did most of the relationship. Asking "why" kept me stuck, so I quit. Well, not so easily. The medicine for this sickness took a long time to work. It had to build up in my system, just like the Program builds in a person.

At first, when I caught myself with a case of the "whys," I applied the mental remedy of gentle understanding. I had the knowledge that asking "why" was not helpful to me, but rather damaging. I had to put a stop to my "whying." Awareness was my key to unlocking my door to good mental health. Since, I had left this "whying" unattended and untreated for so long, it turned into a very contagious and debilitating bad behavior! I noticed how it could spread from one thought on one subject, over to other thoughts – on other parts of my life.

I opened up my awareness and slowly began to catch myself "whying" (either out-loud to a friend), or even more subtle, in my mind. I challenged myself to catch myself when I started asking why. Catching myself became easier over time. I wanted to wash myself of this habit. I no longer wanted to be sick.

My remedies included answering back with antiseptic self-talk.

I applied healthier phrases of:

"It doesn't matter why." or
"I may never know why." (With the additional add-on of, "and it's alright this way.") or
"I don't know what this is all for." (Because I did not hold the BIG PICTURE of all of life's events. Maybe God or The Universe had better romantic ideas for me? Maybe.)

Some of these helped ease my mind. Some of these words calmed the negative voice inside of me. Hearing myself talk, out-loud or in my head, required a commitment to self-care, awareness, and skill. I had to catch myself in the early stages of a sick sentence. Have you ever listened to yourself talk? I found it embarrassing at times. Ugh! Did I really say that!?

In the early days, after ending the relationship with the alcoholic, "whying" contributed to my overall sickness on a daily basis. Each time I asked "why" I could imagine my temperature going up a degree until I was running a high fever of "whys" by the end of the day. I always knew when I had a high "why"-temperature (due to a case of the "whys") because I simply did not feel good. I originally thought processing and figuring things out would make me feel better and help me move forward, but I couldn't have been more wrong! Thinking about it made me think about it more! It became an obsession to know something I couldn't possibly know.

I had to turn my activity of complaining into a better way of expressing myself. I examined myself for more motives and found that during the fragile first months after the broken relationship, I craved continual validation from others that I made the right decision when I ended my relationship. I wanted others to agree with me that the alcoholic was toxic for me while not seeing my own codependent sickness clearly in myself. I yearned for reassurance that I did the right thing by leaving and letting go. Not surprisingly, no one that I called and talked to could satisfy this in the early stage of severe self-doubt. I learned that my longing was only met by giving myself sincere validation and assurance over time. Self-approval on a daily basis is what helped me along.

Even still, I needed support after ending the alcoholic relationship. Friends came in handy, especially Program friends who knew this road. However, not surprisingly, my friends were sick of my obsessive conversations about the alcoholic. So, I attempted to change my daily talking activities regarding my ex. I tried out brief venting sessions with more patient friends who would not allow me to continue asking "why?" The gentle friends in Program meant the most during the withdrawal and the "whys." Sometimes conversations were frustrating. Friends didn't want to go over the same subject (the alcoholic), and I was overly sensitive to being told the truth. Still, I pushed through all the awkwardness of my new intention to stop. One thing was certain: if I was to ever move forward in life, I had to break free of continually asking "why?"

Years later, I got a few answers to my questions. Years later, I began to see reasons I couldn't have thought up or known then. Years later, I understood it all better, after the emotional pain had subsided. Years later, I saw the lessons I learned with the alcoholic as a gift. Years later, I had finally even begun to know "why."

"When we long for life without difficulties, remind us that oaks grow
strong in contrary winds and diamonds are made under pressure."
— Peter Marshall, in prayer

Lesson #7

Be in Reality

False Fantasies

"This above all: to thine own self be true,
And it must follow, as the night the day,
Thou canst not then be false to any man."
— *William Shakespeare, Hamlet*

How did I get so tricked?

I was false with myself, having created a fairy-tale fantasy of a future with the alcoholic. The whole fantasy existed in my mind and daydreams. I wanted life-long happiness with this man. I had visions of laughter, fun, joy, fulfillment, love, romance, and a family with him. The fantasies were dear to my heart. They were my dreams and daydreams on clouds. I think I created the fantasy the day I met him. In my mind, I had built "castles in the sky" with the alcoholic, and I wanted us both to move in!

"Persons appear to us according to the light we
throw upon them from our own minds."
— *Laura Ingalls Wilder*

By the time I had to switch from fantasy to reality, my mental creations, which I had built upon year after year, were over fifteen-years-old. The more I focused on visions of his AA recovery and sobriety, the bigger my fantasies grew, becoming so large that they floated like a giant cloud of denial over my thoughts. Looking back, I realize that I fantasized because I couldn't deal with the pain of the truth and the ugly contradiction that was our reality. He was not in Alcoholics Anonymous. He had no interest in seeking help. Year after year, I learned just how false my fantasies were.

My Lesson #7: Be real with myself and about life

Fantasizing was my way of escaping the truth of my painful situation. I single-handedly tricked myself with my fantasies. I wasn't truthful with myself. The truth was that I didn't like where our relationship was at. I didn't like the relationship I was in. I didn't like the direction my relationship was going. I refused to entertain the logic of my circumstances. (Based on the kind of man that he was acting like; he was not capable of actually living up to the fantasies I had firmly established in my mind.) I was in love my perception of the alcoholic's potential — which really wasn't his potential at all. It was the fantasy of potential that I had dream up for him that kept me waiting around to see if it could happen. What was I waiting to see? Well... I was hoping to see his AA Recovery and his sobriety. I was hoping to see myself happy. I was holding onto the stories of other women who were lucky to experience happiness with a recovering alcoholic in AA. Absurdly, I was holding onto his roller-coaster ride only to see another repeat of his history. My truth of my story was that history, not his promises, became the best predictor of my future with him.

The longer I stayed with him and the more rounds I did in his rodeo, the more I saw the same rotten repeats and reruns. Things eventually fell apart, in about the same time frames, with the same promises, same disrespect, same abuse, and same patterns. Bad attitudes and bad behavior all re-emerged with each chance I gave my alcoholic to be in a relationship with me. I allowed unacceptable behavior towards me over and over, year after year. Consequently, my spirit deteriorated. However, thankfully, my denial also deteriorated. I could no longer pretend that his recovery was just around the corner. When I finally started to despair about him, I shifted my focus to me. **Where was my recovery?**

Tired, exhausted, and worn-out, I asked myself, "Is this the hill you want to die on?" To the credit of my Higher Power, and my soul, I replied back, "No!" I did not want to die climbing the alcoholic's endless hill. I did not want to tie onto his sinking black ship of the pirative, progressive disease of alcoholism and drown along with him. I was willing to stop climbing and wasting my life-force and energy. I wanted to get back to a relationship with me. I was also willing to grab the Al-Anon life-preserver and float in Twelve Step Meetings until I remembered how to swim again.

The diseases of addiction and alcoholism matched perfectly with my codependency. This was my perfect storm. At any moment, a wave of "stinking thinking" or acting-out could crash over us both, and we would both drown in anguish. Going down together was not romantic for me. By the grace of God, I was given a precious little girl to save. Being pregnant made me do the hard work in recovery. A recovery life offered us the promise of a better life. It was a different ship, and it would be steered in a completely different direction.

She wasn't the only little girl to be rescued either. My younger self inside was scared and sinking, too. With my baby's arrival, I found an inner strength that I didn't know I had. It was the strength of a mother. As a mother, I was willing to save her life from this disease, and so my life was saved, too. I became a strong swimmer, unafraid to jump "overboard."

When I was pregnant, I jumped head first into recovery like our lives depended on it. Deep down, I knew my life most certainly did. Looking back, I am so glad that I thought her life was worth saving from this disease. It revealed to me that my life was worth saving, as well. Her presence gave me real hope that we could make it to shore if I let go of the fantasy and lived in reality. Wisdom was now helping me see things as they were, not as they appeared. I asked myself, what was really happening here with the alcoholic? What was really happening with me? Were my dreams just a fantasy? Was continuing to be in a relationship with the alcoholic really being true to myself?

"You can't change an unpleasant reality if you won't acknowledge it.... You can only control what you're willing to face."
— *Karen Marie Moning, Faefever*

Lesson #8

See Yourself Clearly

Sicker Than the Alcoholic

"After a while you learn
the subtle difference between
holding a hand and chaining a soul."
– Veronica A. Shoffstall, After a While

What did I look like?

Thankfully, one day during my bottom, my grandfather, who had been a long-time member in AA, told me something I would never forget: that I was sicker than the alcoholic. I adamantly refused to believe his totally absurd comment! However, I was at my bottom at that time, and I had been there for way too long. When my grandpa said this to me, I sat in shameful shock, immediately feeling angry. Not only was I angry with his message, but I was angry with the messenger too! How could I be sicker than the alcoholic? How could that be what's going on here?

My grandfather knew a lot about alcoholics; after all he was one. So I didn't disregard what he said. Rather I took it into consideration. I mentally chewed on my grandpa's comment for weeks, upset to think he may be right, I stayed away from any more words of wisdom from him. He pointed out to me that though my alcoholic may be acting immature, making bad choices and drinking, I was acting badly, too. Even worse, was that I was not under the influence of any alcohol, yet I was still acting insane. So what was my excuse?

My Lesson #8: I was sick, too

Wow, I thought to myself, Grandpa was right! I was really in bad shape emotionally, financially, and otherwise and I wasn't even using drugs or drinking alcohol! I had my own toxic substances, which included several forms of denial that I regularly practiced to escape the pain. I was blaming the alcoholic for just about everything instead of seeing my part in the mishaps of my life.

I finally came to realize that, indeed, I was sicker than the alcoholic. I was sick with anger, jealousy, low self-esteem, and other things that I didn't realize could even make a person sick. I had no idea that my resentments towards the alcoholic were keeping me sick with a wrathful heart. I had no idea that my thinking, particularly thinking that I could change him, was so unhealthy. I had no idea that my emotional state (crying to get his pity) was unstable and ill. I really never saw myself as being a sick person before my grandfather said that to me. My denial and judgment had allowed me to think I was much better than the alcoholic. I had no idea that holding on and refusing to let go of a man was an indication of an emotionally sick person. I was chaining a soul. Actually, my sickness was chaining two souls. I needed to let go of the alcoholic for my own health reasons.

What I could not deny was reality. I could not deny where my life was being taken by choosing, again and again, to be in a relationship with an alcoholic. I was in subsidized housing again. I was on food stamps again. It was plain to see that choosing him was a bad choice (again). Every time I chose him, I chose sickness.

Even though the choice was unconscious all those times, it was still a choice. One that I regularly made.

> *"Fool me once, shame on you.*
> *Fool me twice, shame on me.*
> *Fool me three times, shame on both of us."*
> — *Stephen King*

Anger

Anger was the first part of those toxic substances that I had to overcome. I was angry with myself for clinging unfailingly to the fairy tale life and fantasy family that I had hoped to have with him. I had to face failure and grieve the loss even if it was fictional. I had to face and deal with my low self-worth and my low self-esteem. I had to work on my issues. I had to build myself up again. I had to make amends to myself. It was not the alcoholic's doing, nor was it his job to fix and fulfill my life. I concluded that it was up to me.

Letting myself continue to be sick in a relationship with an active alcoholic was no longer an option after hitting my bottom. **I learned that I was sicker than the alcoholic.** I knew that a healthy person would not choose to be in an unhealthy relationship, so I had to look at myself. I had to hold up a mirror. I had to come to see myself clearly, that I was indeed sicker than he was. I had to get myself help. And I did. I asked myself, "do I want to stay sick? Or, do I want to get better?"

> *"...with your head up and your eyes ahead*
> *with the grace of woman,*
> *not the grief of a child*
> *and you learn..."*
> – *Veronica A. Shoffstall; After a While*

Lesson #9

Seek a Higher Source

A Higher Power That Wasn't Him

"Sometimes, there is a lot of darkness in this world.
As I see it, you have two choices.
You can be a part of that darkness or you can be the light.
Be the light."
— *Tom Giaquinto*

Who was my Higher Power?

I needed a Higher Power that wasn't the alcoholic. Never did I realize, while revolving around him like a planet around the sun, that I had made the alcoholic my Higher Power. I allowed an alcoholic to run my thoughts, feelings, actions, and dictate my reactions. I lived with his comments and criticisms as if they were the truth of the Universe. I dogged his rantings and applied a cosmic cloud of denial over myself while he purposefully planted words in my mind like seeds. Against myself, I let him keep talking, just to stay in his good graces. I needed a Higher Power that wasn't him. I needed to find my own sun in a different galaxy.

Ever since I was a curious child, staring up at the statues of angels with wings, I had a desire to live a spiritual life and "live in the mystery." I longed for a life filled with awe, amazement, and wonder. I wanted the strength that I saw in women who had a faith in God. I craved a life filled with serendipity, beautiful coincidences, and spiritual signs that felt divinely placed on my path. I wanted holy confirmation that I was right where I was meant to be. I wanted to be glowing in gratitude every day and shine with blessings and abundance. I also wanted the alcoholic to be part of the meaning of my life. Inadvertently, I made the alcoholic my personal purpose, source of love, and my mission.

My Lesson #9: Don't make an alcoholic my Universe or my Higher Power

Although I didn't understand the nature of God — what it was, where it was, who it was, or how He/She/It worked. After trying to play God for the alcoholic, I knew that I was not It. It was clear then as it is clear today: I am not God. Although my upbringing and college years seemed to encourage knowledge, power, and control as ultimate success, my attempts at being master and creator of the Universe only led to an early job burnout in a job that I despised.

God was a mystery to me — one that I wanted solved before I could relax. Someone suggested, "why not just allow God to be an unknown, and live in the mystery?" It seemed wrong to me. I pushed against that uncertainty for years because I wanted concrete evidence and understanding of what exactly God was before I would "buy in." I wanted to know who to pray to and who to yell at. However, a part of me knew that not everything was explainable. I needed to let go of my need to understand everything. This became obvious to me as one of my many "defects of character." I believed it was an asset to be skeptical, which served me well as protection in my past. But this asset had gone astray! Not having a Higher Power had worked against me, especially while I was in a relationship with a disease.

While arguing the notion of a Higher Power for years, I observed that those who believed in one were more peaceful, loving, and happy. I also witnessed those who denounced the idea of a Higher Power lived in fear, negativity, and pessimism. That's how I ultimately made the choice to believe in a Higher Power. It came down to a choice of how I wanted to live, and which was the most appealing option. Which version of a person would I like to be? If it made me happier, peaceful, and strong, why not give it a try even if I didn't understand it all? What I came to learn was that I couldn't get in touch with *my* higher powers until I got in touch with *a* Higher Power.

Turning my life over to a power greater than myself (as Step Three of the Twelve Step Program suggests) was a turning point in my life. It was a key to my real progress in recovery. My "turn-over" was a desperate cry for help to an invisible loving source because I had nowhere else to go when I was alone and five months pregnant with the alcoholic's child. I was stuck with the consequences of my past actions and backed into a corner with no clean way out. I was going to have this baby. Life was inevitably going to be messier from what I thought was my mistake.

I experienced the next long, lonely months as a very scary time of living in the "Unknown." Much of my human power to control what was happening was gone. There was something happening in my womb, that I could not undo (nor do). It was out of my control as to how it was happening, too. I could not manage, supervise, nor direct the creation process of a tiny life-form. The gig was up. I didn't have ultimate control of my life. There was an inner Universe inside of me that I also couldn't control. I found myself in a place of extreme fear.

And I was angry. I hated not having any control. It was such a scary feeling for me. I had to face my uncontrollable "control issues." I looked for someone to blame and kept finding myself at fault. How could I live without control?

After as much fault-finding as I could handle, I found another way. If I believed that a Higher Power had a plan and this was meant to be, then the shift in my thoughts made the current situation a beautiful, obedient waiting period for blessings from a Higher Power. I could surrender serenely if this was all a plan with purpose. One day, sitting in my car, talking to myself about how disappointed I was in myself for getting pregnant, I heard a part of me ask, "what if this child isn't about you?" It was then that a light went on. Maybe a Higher Power wanted this child to be born for reasons I didn't know and couldn't know. Maybe this pregnancy wasn't about me nor was it a mistake. I was taking this too personally. It was then that I woke up from that black hole I had fallen into and shot across the Universe into the mystery. I experience the mystery of birth.

Ultimately, my child became my savior. I realized she was my angel sent from "above" to keep me away from my addiction to the alcoholic. I may have not cared much about how much I was suffering with him; however, I certainly cared whether or not the child suffered from this threefold disease. I wanted my child out of the crossfires of our toxic relationship dynamic. My love for my child motivated me to break my addiction to the alcoholic. The coming child was my cosmic catalyst to reach for something higher than him – a Higher Power.

A big little miracle

When she arrived with a three-day bang, we all stood in awe and wonder of the new-born baby. Even the alcoholic was amazed. The baby seemed to have a special way of silencing us all. The development of a fetus to a baby is a miracle and a mystery of which I have never felt more powerless. The only thing I could do was wait patiently during that time of gestation and take prenatal vitamins. I had to sit in the unknown because there was no other stress-free alternative. Thus, I chose to surrender to a Loving Source versus surrender to my own fears, mental demons, and nagging negativity. Holding her in my arms, skin to skin, I agreed that there was a God or Higher Power in charge and I came to admit that I was not it.

I remember my exact moment of sweet surrender during the pregnancy. I made the decision to turn the surprise pregnancy over as I sat in a passenger seat of a car, driven by a friend taking me to an open Women's AA meeting. I remember the windy, dark stretch of road that we were driving on when I released my will, and finally took a big deep breath. It felt as though I was turning myself over to the spirit of love and deciding not to live in a state of fear any longer. It was not healthy for me to be in a constant state of inner turmoil, nor was that energy healthy for the baby. I was willing to trust Something/Someone/Whoever was out there that I could not see or understand, but came highly recommended.

I was pregnant and confused about the timing of my life events so I went to any meeting available. Friends who believed encouraged me that I was supported by a Higher Power. They said that my job was to feel, believe, and trust that support. At my bottom, I was finally willing to receive help, even if I couldn't get a good solid grasp on God. No one was able to convince me that God existed. Ultimately, I had to experience the nature of God for myself to believe in this Something. To this day, I savor the instant relief I felt wash over me when I surrendered my cares to my Higher Power. I now love doing it. It is one of the most effective actions against alcoholism and co-alcoholism that I take.

Believers told me that with my Higher Power, all things were possible – including ending my addiction to the alcoholic in my life. I had to let go to live, or else hang on to him and die. A believer friend told me that miracles could happen for me when I let go of my sickness and the sick man, using the help of a higher source of strength. At the time, I realized that this could have been my one and only miracle: my ability to let the alcoholic go and to lovingly let myself walk away. It took enormous strength. Strength that I felt didn't come from just me. I had to ask for a Higher Power's help, and I had to borrow a Higher Power's strength.

After that, I found my next challenge. It was frightening for me to walk into freedom. I felt like I had to learn to walk all over again. I had to take one day at a time and one step at a time. At times, I had to do visualizations of holding a Higher Power's hand as I took each step. In my recovery, I reflect on that action being truly a miracle. I became free. Next came the miracle of a healthy baby to hold in my hands. I asked myself, "who will be my Higher Power? The alcoholic or God?"

"God has a Plan. He just works in mysterious ways."
— Unknown

Stage II

In the Cocoon of New Creation

The Chrysalis of Change

(Dealing with spills, self-surgery, and self-containing boundaries.)

...

"We are all butterflies. Earth is our chrysalis."

— *LEEANN TAYLOR*

...

"How does one become a butterfly? They have to want to learn to fly so much that you are willing to give up being a caterpillar."

— *TRINA PAULUS, Hope for the Flowers*

Lesson #10

Love Alone Time

Afraid to Be Alone

*"All transformations are accompanied by
pain. That's the point of them."*
— *Fay Weldon*

Why was I afraid to be alone?

I had another real problem besides the alcoholic: I was afraid
to be alone. I wanted a relationship with someone else, more than
I wanted a relationship with myself. For some reason, I was afraid
of being with myself. There was a deep loneliness at my core that
burned with pain. My codependency wanted to find someone who
could take that away. I battled my loneliness, ran away from it, and
went to the alcoholic to avoid it. It felt like pathological levels of
loneliness combined with a constant craving for connection. My
loneliness was enemy #1.

My Lesson #10: Learn to love my alone time

I experienced the pain of loneliness to be excruciating. I feared
living and trying to survive alone. It was clear to me that I didn't

trust myself nor my abilities. The distrust with myself was not unfounded. Sadly, I had seen myself self-sabotage regularly in plain daylight. I scared myself with my past desperate and destructive decisions which made my fear real.

One lonely day, I pushed aside my facade of self-pride and false confidence, and I was able to be honest with myself: I acknowledged that I was afraid to be alone. I was also afraid to end up alone. I was afraid to look like a lonely living failure. I was afraid, afraid, afraid. I pushed away that fear by acting confident and capable. On the outside, it seemed I had more clarity and more going for me than the alcoholic did (the key word is "seemed"). I was always attempting perfection and trying to do things right. I worked hard, especially in my mind, performing mental overtime. I had to work hard to keep the "look" of things together.

What had happened was my codependency and his alcoholism had robbed me of a sense of self. I had a very weak sense of self, and I did my best to compensate. What I needed was a strong sense of Self to make better choices that would benefit me. In recovery, some people think we have to recover or regain the self that was lost to these diseases. For me, I need to create a sense of self, since I wasn't allowed much of that in my childhood. There wasn't much to recover that would be healthy—perhaps only my light. What I needed to do was create myself. Then I would have some sense of self worth saving.

"In solitude we give passionate attention to our lives,
to our memories, to the details around us."
— Virginia Woolf

To make my matters worse, I was subconsciously seeking a higher person to save me, rather than correctly seeking a Higher Power to help me save myself. I hadn't even embarked on a sojourn to find myself. I just kept trying to find a man. I was seeking "that man"— the "one" that would complete me because I felt like a half a person. I thought that finding love with a man was finding the answer to this nagging fear. I worried about finding love daily.

"Relationshiping" was my high priority hobby, my obsession, and my distraction. Someone told me that resting time is learning time. I didn't know that I wasn't learning and integrating my life's lessons. I refused to rest. I was refusing to be single. Single meant alone.

Friends told me to stop worrying about love. In an effort to scare me out of my love obsession, they said that True Love would only find me when I was healthy and ready for Real Love. They said that the more I suffered over the lack or loss of love from the alcoholic the more I kept Real Love away and at bay. What my closest confidants didn't realize was the extent of my inner starvation: I was starving for attention. I was somehow passively-aggressively attention seeking from others, mostly the alcoholic. I had spent years of my life focusing on my alcoholic and giving him constant attention. What was left of me was silently screaming for attention and love. I didn't know at the time that I need the love to come from myself. Fear didn't push me into True Love. It pushed me to find another person.

With the alcoholic, I was pity-seeking because I knew that was the only way for the alcoholic to notice me, consider me, and feel for me. When I was down on my luck, it felt like the only time he loved me. Sometimes I would get good treatment if I was clearly suffering worse than his regular day's worth of sufferings. I was confusing love with pity then. When the alcoholic would disappoint, I desperately wanted someone to feel sorry for me, and then make it all better. Maybe another man would do the trick (I often thought)?

What I did not know during those starvations was that I was wanting and desperate for the impossible. I wanted someone to make me better on the inside by supplying outside things. I was waiting for someone to cure me of an inner loneliness. Even if I received love, attention, and support from the alcoholic, it had no chance of remedying the ultimate problem inside me. I had a hole inside

59

me to fill that was bigger than anyone could imagine, and it kept getting bigger every day, week, and year in an unfulfilling alcoholic relationship.

The concerning thing I noticed about being in an alcoholic relationship was that I inevitably lost all my close friendships. Being with an alcoholic made me lonelier. One of the many consequences I suffered was the loss of friendships to the disease of alcoholism. Losing all my close friends was an unfortunate by-product of my obsession and focus on an alcoholic. This also made my loneliness real.

In recovery, I was facing loneliness and trying to fix it. I tried many self-help tactics, as well as online dating. (No, online dating is not a form of self-help.) It was a revelation when I heard that the hole I felt on the inside is sometimes called a "holy loneliness." It made me think that loneliness could possibly serve a good purpose. It was described as a natural Spiritual loneliness that drives us to get close with a Higher Power. I didn't feel close with a Higher Power because, in the alcoholic relationship, there was no room for one. I was trying to get close to the alcoholic, who seemed so far away in his own sufferings. I never knew that I could choose to be as close to my Higher Power as I wanted. I never knew that when I was feeling so alone that I had gotten far away from my Higher Power. I now know that loneliness is a signal emotion that tells me I need to reconnect with my Higher Power.

In my worst codependent sickness, I was beyond afraid to be alone I was terrified of it! My sponsor in the Program commented that, in order to truly heal, it may mean being alone. My sponsor also said that, to an extent, I have to do my recovery alone. I was scared to death at the thought. I wanted to hang onto something, someone – especially the familiar people in my life, if things were going to get hard. Looking back over my childhood, I could say that I always felt alone, growing up with my emotionally absent parents. Loneliness was painful, especially to a child. Perhaps, the rebellious child in me was going to use this relationship to never have to feel the pain of childhood loneliness again? Could this be one of those times when my past was creating my future?

The only person in my soul is me

The fear of being alone was a big issue, but I knew that I had other fears to contend with: fears of losing my familiar world and jumping into the always-scary unknown. I had fears of judgment, fears of loss, fears of tears, fears of grief and fears of being swallowed by sorrow. A friend of mine tried to help soften this by explaining that I would be losing an Egoic world but catching up to my Soul world. I had always longed for the authenticity of my soul. My people-pleasing ways of living took me so far away from my own soul over the years that there was a huge gap to bridge. I didn't even know where to begin.

I read something smart somewhere: that the only person in my soul was me. At first, that struck me as such a lonely thought. I wanted others in there too. Holding onto the alcoholic showed me that I was willing to take hostages so my heart had company. Now I can look back as see that that's what I did to the alcoholic, and he was too sick to refuse my capture. I was taking a helpless hostage when I took an alcoholic as a relationship partner.

Profoundly alone

During those early, lonely days after the break-up, another friend pointed out and explained to me that "we are always profoundly alone." She said that I was fighting and resisting something that will always be. She claimed that we are alone in our experience of life because we are the sole perceiver of what is occurring. She believed the theory that we project, like a movie projector, out all the stuff that goes on inside of us, on to our outer lives. I had a feeling she was right. No one could see my life through my eyes exactly.

Accepting the fact that I am profoundly alone in my experiences of the world and always will be, helped soften the lonely loop I was in. This understanding helped my self-doubt. This philosophy she explained applied to everyone. I wasn't just the odd one out with no relationship. I wasn't alone in my aloneness.

One courageous day, I examined my motives of hanging on to the relationship with the alcoholic. My driving factor, my underlying motive for holding on to the sick man, was my fear of being alone. Sadly, that was it: that was my excuse. The sick alcoholic really wasn't a joy to be with anymore. The laughter was gone with him and between us. I had to face the truth. I had to acknowledge that he had an illness. I had to acknowledge that I had one, too. As I held onto him, I became more ill in various, other, strange ways.

I didn't want to be sick anymore, from my stuff nor his. I stretched my mind to imagine a life of freedom from sickness. Wouldn't it be nice if I could face this aloneness straightforward and start living fearlessly and healthily? I gave fearless living a real try when I ended the relationship after fifteen years – on my terms.

Never really alone

During my nine solitary months pregnant, I discovered that I was never really alone when I walked with a Higher Power. The love and comfort I needed for this lifetime were there in my Higher Power. My Higher Power even became the source of a great big reassuring hug I needed so badly. I knew that I could not return to the alcoholic for support. He had none to give, as he had none to give himself.

My problem was that I kept forgetting about a Higher Power. I need to remember a Higher Power was there. Then it was up to me to ask for help, to ask for that hug, even if it was imaginary. During the final months of being pregnant and on the required bedrest, I would envision Jesus wrapping his arms around me while I laid in bed alone with back pain and bleeding. I was "in the mystery" and surrendering myself. I needed to believe in something to get me through the lonely nights of the last trimester. I was always so afraid my water would break, my cell-phone would lose battery power, and my car wouldn't start as soon as labor hit. I prepared for it like the coming of a violent storm. However, fear was being replaced with Faith whenever I imagined that loving embrace at night. I began remembering to pray when things got scary. I began remembering a Higher Power's presence when I felt the surge of loneliness begin, especially at night time.

Willing to be alone

Before I ever tried being alone, it took a real willingness. I had to be willing to face it all. I had to talk myself through the process of not relationship-seeking around every corner. Looking back, the alone time was a time that I built my inner strength and gained enormous clarity. I knew that I could not and did not make good decisions in a state of confusion, and when I was wrapped up in someone else. Clarity was such a grace to receive. I am glad I took that time, even if I was pregnant and sometimes feeling so helpless and scared. It was worth it.

For me, willingness was important to cultivate when I wanted things to change in my life. It was like opening a window to another way – a different perspective when the room filled with black smoke of past negative, fearful, thoughts. When I got scared, I was tempted to reach for people, places, things, and circumstances for security and peace. However, I found over and over again that there was little-to-no-stability in those things. I learned that change is constant in the world. People change, things change, and circumstances change. It was a fact of life. It was the nature of life. It was my error of thinking that I could hold onto people for safety. I needed to trust the flow, grow, change, and mature to keep up with reality. Staying the same wasn't true survival. Standing still was definitely not living. Furthermore, it was painful.

By letting go of the alcoholic, I learned the difference between standing still and stability. It is a known fact that the progressive disease of alcoholism results in terribly unpredictable behavior. There are irrational moments, surrounded by insane thinking, and drunken episodes. My anxiety would build if I tried to control, supervise, hold on, or attach to the alcoholic. Instability with the alcoholic was cyclical, that was something I could count on. I saw the same patterns played out by the alcoholic, and then I saw them in myself, year after year. Basically, I could not count on a sick man. The better question became, could I learn to count on myself?

If I was ever going to count on myself, it would take new ways of being and a new version of me showing up for life. To a certain extent, it would take living fearlessly and free with a whole lot of Faith. I knew I could do a lot of better living with wisdom, patience and a Higher Power. I had to allow the idea of being utterly, despairingly alone to run its course through my overworking mind. I had to be done with the lines of thinking that led me straight back to the alcoholic.

Into myself I go...

I tried to practice meditation. It was through a meditation training that I found the witness self, or the observer within, and I realized there was somehow two variations of me in my mind: one was thinking thoughts and being the perceiver, while the other was watching that perceiver think. So with this I found a second person within me. I made it my task to practice self-observation without judgment.

"The highest form of spiritual practice is self-observation without judgement."
— *Swami Kripalu*

Sometimes, I reached points of awareness where I could hold up a STOP sign and stop my thought stream when a fear-based thought arose. After breaking those inner beatings, I began better self-talk. With a meditation practice, I worked to consciously monitor my thoughts, and catch the bad ones before they went to my emotions or began to tell a sob story about something. I had to monitor my mind. I learned to choose my thoughts as an ability I could cultivate. I had to begin selecting my thoughts every day like I selected my clothes. Occasionally, I was with-it enough to direct thoughts to the opposite of what I was thinking (the more positive alternative). Eventually, I switched my thoughts to that of embracing solitude and serenity. No more did I have to keep reminding myself that I am alone, single, or lonely. I had to remind myself of myself. I had to remind myself of a Higher Power. I had to remind myself of the inner witness. It took years of practice to change the story in my head.

Over time, newer, healthier thoughts of being a vibrant single woman were allowed to enter. Newer thoughts were good for me in so many ways. I was able to create a series of different positive perspectives of how being alone could be fun, freeing, and fantastic for me. What would I be doing if I were alone? How would I feel if I didn't worry about someone else's impending doom and destruction? How free would I feel if I let go and allowed him to live his life as he saw fit? How relieved would I be to be unattached to what progressive alcoholism brings? How much more simpler could my life be? Could even fun return to my life?

Solutions to loneliness

Loneliness was solved through connection. I connected to myself, Program friends, and a Higher Power. After telling myself a new story about what being alone and single meant, who could be afraid of being alone? I decided (made a decision — like Step Three suggests of the Twelve Steps) to tell a new story about being a single woman and what that meant. My new storyline turned the self-abusive shame around. I came to find that being alone was nothing to be afraid of, even if I felt moments of fear. I was always with my thoughts. I was always with my Higher Loving Self if I chose. If remembered, I could always feel surrounded and watched over by a Higher Power. I practiced making my thoughts friendly, supportive, and affirming. I asked my Higher Power to join me in my life as a co-creator of my newly formed life of freedom, joy, and love. I asked for help. I prayed for daily guidance. I shifted to thinking that I was not actually choosing to be alone when I left the relationship but instead choosing to be with myself. I made the effort to choose to be with myself and create a better self. I chose to connect with a loving Higher Power verses an alcoholic suffering man. I ended the relationship with the alcoholic. When I left, I began a relationship with me. How could I learn to love my alone time?

"Inside myself is a place where I live all alone and that's where you renew your springs that never dry up."
— Pearl Buck

Lesson #11

Be Angry

"Anybody can become angry - that is easy, but to be angry with the right person and to the right degree and at the right time and for the right purpose, and in the right way - that is not within everybody's power and is not easy."
— *Aristotle*

Who was I angry at?

I felt angry with him, at him, because of him, and for him. For most of the relationship, all of my anger was directed towards the alcoholic. Anger spewed out of me, whether I was talking or not. My angry silences were solid attempts to punish him as much as my harsh words could. At one point, disgusted with my state, I said to myself, "you wouldn't feel so angry and be so busy building resentments, if you took better care of yourself!" And I was right!

If I started putting myself first, if I began choosing for me every time, and if I attempted living each day for me, I knew it would make a difference in my negative attitude and lower my anger levels.

I would stop the crazy creation process of finding more things to be angry about with the alcoholic.

The point was that I was angry. I was angry with him, myself, my circumstances, Life, and God. I understood, after taking an introductory psychology class, that the worst thing I could do with my anger was not to feel it. Rather than push anger away, I had to come to identify anger as a signal emotion. My awesome anger was telling me something; it was telling me about something important happening or not happening in my life. Some of the events that triggered my anger were going on under the surface of the alcoholic events and were sometimes too subtle to be seen. To begin dissolving my anger, I needed to validate my anger, have other people hear about it, and validate me too. I needed come into allowance with the part of me that was feeling angry. I needed to allow myself to be angry.

My Lesson #11: Allow myself to be angry

I declared I was angry. I admitted to myself that I was sick with anger. I unearthed the belief I held that it was wrong or bad to be angry. Where did I learn that? When I questioned myself about my hang-ups with anger, I discovered that I was mostly angry because I was angry. This, along with someone pointing that fact out to me, helped me understand that I was angry with myself!

When I explored the deeper elements of anger itself, I discovered that anger had vigorous and vital energy. I found that the energy attached to anger had enough of a charge for this woman to create positive changes for herself. Anger, as I felt it, was not a stale emotion. I noticed that anger did not vibrate on the same energetic wavelength as hopelessness and despair. Anger had heat, fire, and plenty of fuel to last the night. Becoming keen to this emotion and its components took practice. Harnessing this awesome anger for good in my life took mindfulness. Eventually, I learned to utilize anger for its energetic quality. I began to see that anger could be used

in a good way to have a positive impact on my life. Anger held the
energy potential for change.

"When angry, count to four; when very angry, swear."
— *Mark Twain*

I discovered that healthy expressions of anger cleansed me. It
was a purge whenever I spilled my long list of anger towards the
alcoholic to a trusted friend in Program. Anger became my ally and
was helpful in setting boundaries with myself and others. It gave me
the guts to say "NO MORE!" to the disease of alcoholism. It gave
me enough wherewithal to get angry if I was falling into self-doubt
again. I kept in mind and considered the important uses of anger
when it arose. After all, I had to get "good and angry" to be able to
leave.

Over time, I identified that anger was also a helpful tool in
remembering past pain. The anger that I felt when I recalled feelings
of betrayal helped me make my amends to myself. It kept me on
the path of being good to myself. Angry recollection also served as
prevention in keeping other toxic and destructive people out of my
life. I began to see that anger had its beneficial uses.

In therapy, I affirmed that I had a right to feel angry. I soon
learned to give myself permission to feel all of my anger. I allowed
myself to feel angry because if I masked it with stand-in feelings such
as sadness and tears, it did not help. Anger repression kept me stuck.
I was bleeding power, dignity, and self-respect by denying my right
to feel angry. I had a right to feel my anger. I also had a right to feel
and release the emotion properly. I found out that I could own my
anger without accusations, blame, or apologies. It became simply a
feeling, a feeling that I learned to honor.

Thus I began to cherish anger. The anger pushed me forward.
It kept me stirred up to care about myself. Anger didn't defeat
me, it advanced me. Anger stopped being a setback for me when
I embraced it with thankfulness, and then anger was a set-up for

me to take a better path. It was the internal opposition I needed; it was a negative forced I used for my good. It supplied me with determination.

I began to identify that, when my anger turned inward, it led me right into feeling shame and depression. I experienced that my anger lost its authentic, awesome energy for change when I directed it at myself. In the past, I was afraid of anger's outward expression. I felt nervous that my buried anger could burst into an uncontrollable rage. I worried that it would be harmful to me and others. Mostly, I was afraid of being embarrassed by my potential angry outburst. Fear of further embarrassment made me keep loads of anger in me. Also, I didn't want my anger or rage to be a destructive force in my life. I took inventory of the results of my rage. I witnessed that a full-blown rage wouldn't back off until the other person was hurt too. In that scene, no one won, and everything that had to do with goodwill towards man was destroyed with rage. There would be emotional hangovers and a fall-out, including a sense of personal failure where I would then hate myself for raging. In order for waves of anger to dissipate, I had to feel my true feelings, express it accurately, learn to articulate it to a safe witness, and talk about the truth of the events of my life. I needed a safe witness; I needed my anger witnessed.

Speaking my truth was what shifted my anger to allow my other emotions to surface afterwards. Anger was a cover-up emotion. It essentially blocked out every other feeling that I didn't want to feel. Learning to express my feelings about an anger-producing incident lightened and enlightened me. All the years spent with an active alcoholic in my full-blown codependency gave me plenty to be angry about. It was an incredible transfer when all the energy I used to keep my anger contained was released for me, and I simply let myself feel it. I learned to feel without trying to fix (or doing something about) that feeling. I discovered that after I had allowed myself to express anger healthily, I had more energy. I needed healing for myself, buried under layers of my angry protection. Somehow anger protected me. I began to feel how much sadness I felt because of the alcoholic's disrespectful behavior towards me. I began to feel how regretful and sad I was that I had let myself down.

With practice, I learned not to spend all my energy protecting myself from the disease. Instead, I would set a boundary, or I would be called to set a stronger boundary if necessary with the alcoholic. I began preventing more anger in my life with boundaries. I never realized how much of my energy was being used by my defenses until I set strong enough boundaries with people who would drain my energy and invade my personal space with their drama.

Boundaries helped me protect just what my life was really all about. I became more free, stable, and centered in my own life. Setting firm boundaries around the actions I would not accept from myself and others influenced all of my relationships; not just the tumultuous one with my alcoholic. When I practiced boundaries, my life took on more definition. I began to know who I was more and more each day. I stepped more fully into my personal power. Time and energy were freed for my chosen pursuits. People gained respect for me. Some people even began to fear the sensitive and sweet little me! I soon realized that what they feared was not me, but the Truth. With permission to feel my anger, I was able to tell others about it. Venting sessions were valuable.

It was a real "win" for me when I refused to wait around for better behavior from an ill, toxic, and defiant alcoholic man. That one decision set me free from so much anger. It was a boundary with myself that prevented more things for me to end up angry about. I also learned how important it was to inform others when I was feeling angry or if something mattered to me. Giving people accurate information created a potential for others to change their behavior in response. When I began to express anger in a direct, healthy, way with boundaries, I learned some things about myself, too. I got a new slant on my old relationship problems. It led to accessing crucial memories of past disrespect that had been banished to the shadows with my denial. I even discovered the more subtle ways in which I inadvertently set up certain problems for myself. This awareness through anger gave me abilities to do better for myself next time, and every time.

Releasing my anger and speaking my truth made a real difference for me. Changing other people was not my primary reason for expressing the anger. My motives were about sparing and saving me from storing anger. The primary reason for giving a voice to all the things I was angry about was that they were there, and they were my truths as I experienced them. I learned that like any other feeling, expressing anger is a great release. I allowed anger to surface and release not to change someone, but for me.

As I allowed myself to have my anger, things began to change with the alcoholic. I no longer believed that feeling angry made me a bad person. To my delight, my ex once wrote me a parenting note and slipped in a sentence that I was intimidating to him. I thought that was lovely to hear! I went from a doormat, people-pleasing, nice, sweet, quiet, and reserved girl to being feared for my new ability to call bullshit! I felt like my insides went, "YAY!" when I read that note. Previous to all the self-work I had done, I would have been devastated to have read this about myself. I would have thought I did something wrong and would apologize profusely.

As I refined my anger awareness, I began to see other benefits of anger. From my anger study, I went forward setting boundaries, thereby dissolving my continual need to always be on the defensive. I allowed myself to feel the emotion and sit with it, rather than act on it in a heated frenzy. I noted that big emotions always passed. If emotions weren't ruling me, if I wasn't "emotionally hijacked" by them, I knew I would make it. It is called emotional sobriety. By accepting this formerly feared emotion of anger, I was paving the way for my world to improve, to have fulfillment in my life and carry out my mission.

Besides a signal emotion, I learned that anger is spiritual. It brought me closer to my Higher Power, even if I was yelling. It made me connect to the infinite. I got closer to the truth of things. I learned that anger was good if it helped to build rather than destroy.

So I used it to build a bridge to a Higher Power's love and resources. Hey, it opened up the channels of communication. I asked myself, "how can I use my anger for good?" For me, I used anger to build a new life for myself.

> *"Bitterness is like cancer. It eats upon the host. But*
> *anger is like fire. It burns it all clean."*
> *— Maya Angelou*

Lesson #12

Be Willing to Be Alone

How Loneliness Became Good for Me

"Loneliness is the poverty of self; solitude is the richness of self."
— May Sarton

What's good about being alone?

After the bouts of loneliness, abandonment, and feeling unimportant to the alcoholic and the world, I resurfaced. It is amazing how just a simple shift to a new perspective would get me thinking the opposite. I used to think that loneliness was bad for me until I discovered its great benefit. Feelings of loneliness drove me to search-out, and connect with a Higher Power. I found myself when I was alone. Maybe I was searching for myself all along?

It was in my most desperate moments when I truly asked for help and love from a different source. No longer could a sick and suffering alcoholic be my comforter in times of grief. Actually, he walked out, and I had to seek out a Higher Power. I also had to seek out myself.

My Lesson #12: Being alone is good for me

When my first grandfather passed away, death was a big deal to me. He was the first death experience of a loved one, other than pets, that I had ever faced. In my attempts to seek sympathy, I contacted the alcoholic, whom I had just broken up with. I justified my action by telling myself that we had been together so long and he knew me and my family the most. He, of course, loving to be a hero in any type of excitement, came to the rescue. He offered me a meal and a place to stay. I was grateful for a place to go and a person on the other end of the line. I didn't want to face death alone.

However, relying on him was my error. I had better choices, though I didn't make them. I asked my alcoholic for help with my grief, when he, had more unresolved grief of his own. I asked someone who was emotionally handicapped himself to help me with my emotions. He came through as a person who felt drawn to the drama of death and the self-pity in my voice.

After a warm meal and a place to stay with the alcoholic, I ultimately had to face death and grief on my own. What I didn't know at the time was that my contacting him, rather than choosing a trusted friend, would change the course of our lives forever. My moment of desperation started a chain reaction that neither one of us could ever reverse. I didn't know it at the time — actually not until three months later, not until I had written the volcanic eruption of wisdom in the first part of my book on leaving him – that I had become pregnant on that night. I spent years blaming him for what he could not do, only to end up doing something unconscionable myself. I woke me up to my part in the dysfunction codependent-alcoholic dance.

None of my actions were planned. My motives were as pure as needing someone who cared and someone to cry with. That was how I ultimately forgave myself. In reflection, my loneliness drove me to drive down the wrong street that night. Desperation and big emotions tended to do that to me. I needed to examine my compulsions, my impulsive decisions, my lack of self-care, my lack of self-worth, my neediness, my inability to handle reality mentally, and my delusions. What was going on inside of me already that a death in the family brought to light?

Could I have gone to a Higher Power during that moment of pain and not someone who was also suffering? Could I have called any other friend? Yes, but I was still "hoping to find the bread in the hardware store." I had hoped that maybe this time he could come through for me and it would last. I secretly desired that he would come out of his self-centered disease and put me first. I wanted the love and attention that I didn't get from him, and damn it, I now finally had a reason to cry for it. Truth is, I really hadn't let completely go when I was still hoping to get something from him.

After a few years of loneliness like no other, that of being alone and pregnant through the entire nine-month term, then alone with a colicky baby, I could examine loneliness with different glasses on. I used to look at being alone like it was a death to avoid. I would avoid being lonesome by keeping busy, getting involved, having a romantic interest, and basically running. I spent years doing that, and it never worked. I came to a realization that I had to embrace loneliness as a human emotion that needed to be felt. I was lonely no matter what. I was lonely in a relationship. I was lonely with a child, which I thought would solve the answer to my chronic loneliness but didn't. I was lonely even while working a job I loved. I was lonely even with good friends. I was a lonely, love addict woman.

> *"Negative emotions like loneliness, envy, and guilt have*
> *an important role to play in a happy life; they're big,*
> *flashing signs that something needs to change."*
> — *Gretchen Rubin*

It dawned on me that the loneliness was a longing for connection and it could be a good thing. It may be the catalyst: the thing that creates a desire to learn, grow, and connect. I had to change my thinking. Loneliness could be a good thing for me when recognized, and if I met it with gentle understanding. It could be a good thing when it connected me to a Higher Power and myself. How unconnected was I with my own thoughts, feelings, and desires? Could loneliness be called solitude and not loneliness?

My shift in perspective lightened the whole concept. I learned that I may never stop feeling this emotion. Rather, it could be used to drive me to seek myself as a source of compassion or seeking out my loving Higher Power. It would ultimately be the factor that made me take a step off the edge to believe in a power greater than myself.

I started to believe in myself when I would make it months, then a year, without someone, especially the alcoholic. These were my new anniversaries. I found myself in the void. I found myself in peaceful solitude. I could finally hear my inner voice since the alcoholic wasn't around for me to listen to. Now that I was alone, practicing solitude, could I finally self-partner?

"Loneliness expresses the pain of being alone and
solitude expresses the glory of being alone."
— Paul Tillich

Lesson #13

Make Boundaries, Say "No!"

Bold Boundaries Are a Must!

"Saying no can be the ultimate self-care."
— *Claudia Black*

Did I have any boundaries?

Setting and establishing boundaries with the alcoholic, came only after I made a firm and final decision to care for myself. Before I could "boundary set" with any success, I had to truly decide to take care of myself. I also had to make a clear decision to end the relationship with him as completely as possible. By setting boundaries, I took charge of my life and the direction my life was going to take. I used the familiar words and told myself "My Higher Power helps me when I help myself!" So I did.

My Lesson #13: Make myself some boundaries, say "No!"

I realized that creating boundaries around myself was my job, just like taking care of myself had become my new full-time job. I was on a self-empowered-driven mission to finally help myself out. Self-preservation had to take precedence over saving him or saving the stale relationship. I realized that some of my escape plans had to involve setting boundaries with a man who was not used to such treatment. Deep down, I knew and feared that there would be backlash to deal with, due to me standing up for myself and him not getting his way. I hesitantly started by using the strongest boundary word out there; "No." After some practice, I tried to make it a bit more loving by saying, "No Thank You," occasionally, too.

> *""No" is a complete sentence."*
> *— Anne Lamott*

After setting the first boundary with the alcoholic, I soon learned that I had to make boundaries – and lots of them. To my dismay, the tough challenge was not over once I set a boundary. I became very aware that I would have to reinforce my boundaries with him on numerous occasions. I also noticed the feelings of guilt that were stirred up in me when I took an action that was new for me. I learned to breathe through all of the uncomfortableness I felt after boundary-setting. Initially, I experienced a lot of tears setting boundaries. Looking back, I realized the tears were part of my breakthrough.

Boundaries with myself?

I spent months studying boundaries to get an understanding of why they were so important. Just what was a boundary anyhow? I searched several resources on the topic. I was serious about getting better and about my recovery. The most frightening awareness I had during my research was that I had very little boundaries with myself! This completely changed the way I understood boundaries. No longer was I just focused on setting boundaries with others, I turned to face myself. I had to take myself "on." It was disappointing to realize that once I set a boundary with myself, I often crossed it either without realizing it or with some impulsive justification I used as an excuse. This awareness launched a new way of setting boundaries. I had to start by setting them entirely with myself!

I reflected and realized that all my prior attempts at setting boundaries with my alcoholic failed. Why did I expect him to respect my boundaries outside of the relationship when he never respected me in the relationship? Why was I expecting him to respect my boundaries when I didn't fully respect my own with myself? I experienced an "Ah-ha" moment uncovering my crazy expectations about boundaries. So I began to ask myself two big questions: "where was I crossing my own boundaries?" and "what boundaries could I not maintain in my life?" I didn't like some of the answers I came up with. I was then able to see my part in my own misery.

Through self-observation and enough time with myself, I recognized that my spirit was starting to die from the lack of limits I maintained for myself and from total enmeshment with my alcoholic. There were no boundaries. The ones that were left standing were withering under the pressures of the advancing disease like an ever-increasing wind. My boundaries blew over very easily.

Boundaries were no little thing. I realized that I was single-handedly diluting the power of my life by failing to set boundaries. I came to believe that it was not selfish of me to protect things that mattered, like my time on this Earth. This mainly included the amount of time I spent in my mind focused on him. I was bleeding power daily because I was unable to stop thinking about him, even with no-contact with him. It did seem that my mind wanted to go over and, over and, over everything that was unsettling that had to do with him. I had no boundaries with myself over how much time I spent on him in my mind. Where were my mental boundaries? I had none. I would think about him anywhere, with anyone, and all the time. It was quite evident in my talking and daily dialogue with my Sponsor.

The use of distractions

Once I began to realize the importance of where I was spending my mental energy daily, I had to start setting boundaries with myself. I started to tell myself to stop thinking and to stop focusing on him. However, I crossed that boundary time and time again. I realized I couldn't stop obsessing about him. It was an automated habit by now for my mind to think about him, and my mind was seemingly uncontrollable. At first, the only way I was able to distract my obsessive mind was through the use of distractions. I used mental distractions like movies, romance novels, exploring new-age things as a way to stop thinking about the alcoholic so much. I used distraction because I was so unsuccessful at first with setting boundaries with myself that I continually kept crossing. I would declare that I would not talk about him for the day, and to my dismay, I would have had several ongoing conversations about him and the past with anyone who would listen. In an effort to support my addiction, friends unwilling to listen were not on my call list. They had boundaries of their own and were completely done listening to the same old stories and reruns about the alcoholic. I now think they were smart to shut me off. However, so were the people that helped me process the stories a few hundred times more— until my mind was finally done and was ready to tell a new story.

"When we fail to set boundaries and hold people accountable, we feel used and mistreated. This is why we sometimes attack who they are, which is far more hurtful than addressing a behavior or a choice."
— Brené Brown, The Gifts of Imperfection: Let Go of Who You Think You're Supposed to Be and Embrace Who You Are

I really wanted to know how I was going to get healthy and then hold onto good health. The answer came loudly from *within me,* "you are going to have to make boundaries with him and especially yourself." Then, I heard my newly acquired common-sense mind speak back, "and yes, of course, he won't like it. But remember it's not about him anymore! This is about saving yourself."

Over a short period of time, boundaries started to keep me sane, healthy and protected. I learned that a boundary is a limit that promotes integrity. My integrity was at stake when I didn't set or keep boundaries for myself or with him. I knew deep down that my soul was keeping track of my integrity. By the limits I started setting, I protected the integrity of my day, my energy, my spirit, my health, my heart, and my life. Every day of my life was being shaped by my choices. Clearly, I needed to make better choices. Setting boundaries became a choice I needed to make often. I changed my way of thinking, I changed what I was doing, and it changed my life. I set boundaries so that I could finally have a life. And then I asked myself, where else did I need boundaries?

"Every woman that finally figured out her worth, has picked up her suitcases of pride and boarded a flight to freedom, which landed in the valley of change."
— Shannon L. Alder

Lesson #14

Set Some Boundaries

Making Boundaries to Be Fair to Myself

"Courage is fear that has said its prayers."
— *Dorothy Bernard*

Can I safely set boundaries?

At last, there came a tipping point in which I was screaming inside to myself: "if you are going to set boundaries – set them!" I learned once again that words are not action. Words are just words. I used to worry about the alcoholic's words, but I had my own words to take a look at. Understanding that I had been violated was a first step towards knowing I needed to set a boundary. Understanding that I had allowed the violation was the second step. Doing something about it was my third.

What I found out "the hard way" was that "half-boundaries" did not avail me of the better conditions I wanted. The saying "half measures avail us nothing" from AA applied to me, too, in Al-Anon. Similarly, half-boundaries didn't avail me of half-abuse or half-a-feeling of being dumped on. I found that half-measures still resulted in allowing a confused man to continue to do what he was always doing to me – dumping his anger, guilt, self-pity, and hatred on me. I was still allowing my confused self to take on things that weren't mine. I wasn't being fair to myself.

Lesson #14: Set boundaries with myself!

I had previously made a firm commitment to myself that I intended to keep – I refused to hold onto any excuse to stay in an emotionally abusive environment/relationship. Thus, I began to question my part in it. How much of the emotional abuse was my doing (to me)? Was I emotionally abusing myself by being in the relationship? I finally grasped and admitted to myself that if I stayed with my alcoholic, it would be for all the wrong reasons. I held onto hope that on the other side of changing myself and my life, there was a possibility of my happiness.

I made new vows; this time to myself. I vowed that the next time I entered into a relationship, the very first time that special someone tried to dump their feelings on me, I would set a boundary. I would refuse to engage in their sounding board strategy to hook me into their corrupt conversation. I called this "the spill." It was like a contaminated emotional overflow. I no longer wanted to be infected with my partner's bad moods, nor allow his feelings, confusion, or problems to be poured onto me. How many times did my alcoholic walk away smiling, after leaving me with his frown? My answer was: every time. If he had found that I was willing to listen and absorb his bad feelings, he took advantage of that. No wonder he felt better AFTER talking to me! I was being a container for his problems.

The alcoholic must have felt some relief while I was playing the role of "Miss Fix-It," because the uncomfortable energy (and thoughts) were now in my mind and body. How many times did I volunteer to be the victim of the "let me listen to your problems and take them on emotionally as my own?" Sadly, a lot. How was this fair to me?

"We need to have a talk on the subject
of what's yours and what's mine."
— Stieg Larsson, *The Girl with the Dragon Tattoo*

In rebellion, I attempted to build my verbal skills to stop people from transferring their bad feelings on to me. I stopped joining them in their anxiety and learned to hang up the phone. I no longer accepted sarcasm or any comment that was demeaning, degrading, or undermining. And let me tell you there were lots of opportunities for it in my old life! I hung up the phone a lot. I also learned to "hang-up" on myself when all those toxic things were coming from my end of the "phone." I learned that if I listened longer than the first insult, I was allowing the behavior. I began the practice of deleting texts and emails almost as fast as they arrived. My courage grew. I made it through the uncomfortable emotions of tuning out the people who broadcast crap! I stop broadcasting my own crap.

"The only real conflict you will ever have in your life won't be with
others, but with yourself."
— Shannon L. Alder

I had to mentally eject many bogus "tapes" (claims) by the alcoholic. Even if he claimed (and even if I still carried the illusion) that I was the only one who understood him, that I was the only one who could save him, or that my love could heal him, I had to remind myself that those stories were just that – stories, not facts. They were stories created out of fantasy and false hope. By the time I realized that I couldn't do enough to fix him or help him, I had lost parts of myself, and I wanted myself back.

I had to be careful not to put the notion of "being fair" to him over my own safety or mental health of being fair to myself. I didn't want to get re-trapped into the thinking that my alcoholic partner deserved one more chance. I knew for sure, after the last round, that my love would not heal him. I knew deep inside that there would be no more chances with me because there was almost no more me to have a chance with.

I thought about the whole concept of chances. Chances in-and-of themselves indicated a major problem. Another chance meant logically another chance for major problems. My common sense sharpened and I finally accepted reality. I was done. Done with the disease's words and promises. Done with giving the disease more chances. Done with the painful codependent relationship. Done.

I finally learned the lesson through the extreme amounts of pain. Any association with the alcoholic sent the warning alarms off inside me. No longer was there a thrill or a hope attached to his name. No longer was there a fantasy. The disease had progressed, and now my body responded with sickness when having him even in my energy field. Hearing his name sent waves of sadness, grief, and warning. I was on my way to health when my internal responses matched my past experiences of him and not the fantasy of what I wanted. I set the boundary with myself: no more hurting me, by using or being involved with him. This was me finally being fair to myself. I wiped myself off, learned to sit elsewhere, and found places without phones that would ring. I also changed my number. How else could I be fair to myself?

"Sooner or later in life, we will all take our own turn being in the position we once had someone else in."
— Ashly Lorenzana

Lesson #15

Get Ready to Go Inwards

Getting Ready to Set Boundaries

"Daring to set boundaries is about having the courage to love ourselves, even when we risk disappointing others."
— *Brené Brown*

Was I slowly dying in the alcoholic relationship?

I certainly was spilling life-force energy into the alcoholic situation. It was a slow bleed; my power was being sucked out of me and I stood there watching as it was siphoned by alcoholism. Mental health experts claimed that boundaries were a necessary part of healthy living, and now I believed them. I learned that violating my own boundaries, or allowing someone else to violate them, would cause my energy and spirit to spill out of myself and my life. Without boundaries, I felt drained. Admittedly, I had failed to set boundaries even with myself. And sadly, I let my alcoholic walk all over my boundaries from time to time. I was too weak, drained, and dehydrated to resist. I needed to perform some "self-surgery" soon, or my soul would surely die.

My Lesson #15: I must go inwards to "stop the bleed"

I felt uneasy when I learned that healthy boundaries are meant to be flexible and fence-like. In the past, before I became boundary savvy, I was so afraid of breaking because I bent so much. Cement, concrete, and fortress-like boundaries were my "go-to" behavior for my "safe-mode." I knew that building cement walls for boundaries was not the act of an emotionally strong person. After years of doing it the old way, the hard way, I learned that boundaries needed the extra ingredient of balance, too. I learned that balanced boundaries were meant to let the good in as well as keep the bad out. But from where I was, in critical condition, I needed to operate on my life with strong boundaries first.

For a while, I fought the idea of flexible boundaries. I wanted things to be easier as to when to set a boundary than having to make daily, hourly, and sometimes moment-by-moment judgment calls in the ever-so-confusing "grey areas of life." I wanted clear-cut options: black and white, right and wrong, easy and hard. I wasn't a fast-on-my-feet doctor, so I craved the instant relief that I felt on the other side of an impenetrable stone wall, which no man and no disease could get through. After finding out that blocking out everyone and everything did not serve me well in the long-run (because from a blocked place no one was able to help me), I was willing to take a balanced approach to boundary setting. I wondered if my ingrained survival skills and coping mechanisms would even allow me to make fences. I had found yet another area for personal growth. However, I needed a hospital bed first and some convalescences.

"No good ever comes from putting up walls. What people mistake for safety is in fact captivity. And few things thrive in captivity."
— Louise Penny

Boundary experts explained over and over again that good healthy boundaries allow the positive things in while keeping the harmful things out. I certainly didn't want to miss out on the good things in life. I was already doing too much of that, bed bound from the breakup! For me, boundaries became more than just a decision to stop certain things. I realized that boundaries could also provide a clear moral compass, set as a way to keep me on track and be able to go places. This new concept meant living my life with a focus, creating good rules for myself to go forward with, and more structure in my life. I started to see that I was unknowingly hurting myself when I gave my time and my life to pursuits that didn't match my own morals and values. In my past, for the relationship, I had given up a lot of my time to things that I didn't want. I learned that when I said "No" to him, it was like saying "Yes" to me.

My time

After all the debilitating years in a boundary-less relationship, I felt a strong need to protect my time. I looked over my mental medical chart, so to speak. I could no longer allow the minutes of my life to be "vacuumed up" by the needs of others (or time with others). They would surely sip my life-blood if I let them. And truth be told, I was now too aware to consciously violate myself now without feeling the immediate discomfort of offending myself. When I got sick, I became more sensitive to slips. If I slipped, I then had to do the extra work of having to make amends to myself. It was better to not allow myself to fall and get sick in the first place because each health issue used up my sick days and took more of my precious time. I lost years of my life to other people's repeating dramas, especially my alcoholic partner. I intimately understood that my suffering was the result of going along in his bad direction. I wanted to take my own direction. I wanted a healthier future.

I noticed positive shifts as I began practicing boundaries in regard to my time. By doing this seriously, I began to limit exposure to uncaring people. As a good consequence, I had time to nurture contacts with people who had the potential to become great assets to me. The good things became available to me because I became clear and committed to establishing boundaries. I used my power of choice. I chose wellness.

> *"Evaluating the benefits and drawbacks of any relationship*
> *is your responsibility. You do not have to passively*
> *accept what is brought to you. You can choose."*
> *— Deborah Day, Be Happy Now!: Become*
> *the Active Director of Your Life*

Possibilities began to open up in my life, since setting boundaries gave me more time for the person who needed me most – me! After going about the business of my life so mindlessly before, by setting small boundaries, I started to appreciate the value the little decisions in life, too. Little boundaries that I put in place added up to big rewards. I set boundaries around myself on what I would and would not do, or how much of it. I recognized that even small decisions had the potential to use up my time and my life significantly. I learned how to have a date with me!

Blocking out and letting in

I practiced boundary-setting with others and the alcoholic. It took more courage and emotional strength than I had anticipated. Boundaries with others let them know who I was and where I stood. I needed boundaries to protect the tender parts of myself. Standing up for myself by carving out boundaries with others was a very new behavior. Thus, things were very uncomfortable at first in my new skin. Setting boundaries gave me the opportunity of letting people in who would become meaningful to me. My newly established boundaries freed up time for those people who would eventually really matter to me in a positive way and help me grow. I could see that when I began to limit my exposure to one toxic person (namely the alcoholic), it gave me time to spend with healthier people. In this way, boundaries began preventing further harm, and at the same time gave me health benefits.

With constant practice, I became more versed in boundaries, limits, and deal-breakers. Good healthy boundaries protected my time and energy so that I could fill up my life with things that were truly important to me. I changed the direction of my life-force flow. With boundaries, less was being spilled out, and my body was catching up by making its new supply and keeping it contained. Not surprisingly, I could function better in life with a full supply of myself.

I was the only one who could change my life for the better. No one was going to block out the bad things in my life for me. There was no doctor to detect this. There was no physician with a prescription for living in an alcoholic relationship. There was no IV they could give me in the emergency department to replenish what was being drained. Most often, crises like these don't show up on the CAT scan, but I knew they were there somewhere inside of me. Sadly, sometimes they did show themselves. I learned that sometimes these internal troubles caused actual physical ailments. I even had to undergo real surgery. I knew it was from stress, and I knew where my stress was from.

My life began working for me when I managed my time according to my own healthy sense of how to arrange things in my life. I certainly wanted a better experience of life, and setting boundaries was a huge step toward having those experiences. I had to prepare my own home "operating table" by plugging up, sealing off, and clamping holes, and putting a boundary between myself and the alcoholic. I performed surgery on my life with boundaries in place. My main question became: what boundaries did I need to set with myself first?

"Boundaries are, in simple terms, the recognition of personal space."
— Asa Don Brown, The effects of childhood
trauma on adult perception and worldview

Lesson #16

Set Boundaries with Yourself

Personal Boundaries of Protection

*"The boundary to what we can accept is
the boundary to our freedom."*
— Tara Brach, Awakening from the Trance of Unworthiness

Can I tell myself, "No"?

I learned to tell myself "No" with wisdom. My personal boundaries had to expand and evolve beyond just telling the alcoholic "No!" I discovered that I needed emotional boundaries, physical boundaries, mental boundaries, physiological boundaries, etc... to stay centered and sane. I needed boundaries within myself, enforced by my morals, values, standards, and strong sense of self. I needed to seal up all the holes in my life (and mind) where the alcoholic infiltrated my system without these ever-so-important-to-put-and-keep-in-place boundaries! Even more so, I needed boundaries against my own fearful reactions and his obvious attacks on my recovery. I had to make decision by decision, grounded in the guidance from my gut, backed by myself and my Higher Power.

My Lesson #16: Set boundaries with myself (and others)

Lack of personal boundaries led to me living a life of walking on the eggshells of others. I also walked around my scary-sharp emotions, too, in an attempt not to feel them. For over a decade, I was him-focused and not "me-focused." Looking back, I can see that I was always partnering with the alcoholic and not self-partnering. After setting the first boundaries with the alcoholic and myself, while feeling extremely uncomfortable and vulnerable doing so, I recognized that it would require a lot of work on my discipline of character to walk flat-footed and self-partnered the rest of this "recovery road."

Mistakes happen. Sometimes I had a misstep. Sometimes I slipped and broke a bone and a boundary. I uncovered that even if I "blew" a boundary, I found the alcoholic remarkably responsive to consequences. I created a consequence of being unavailable to him and he caught on (and only sometimes would forget). Personally, I decided to be unavailable to lies. It was a boundary I set up for myself, with myself. I learned the hard way about the various ways a person can and does lie. This included my ways and his ways. I became educated in the manipulative tactics of keeping me (a controlling codependent) in the dark. I decided that failure to disclose important information or not telling me the information which I would have been interested in knowing (because the information matters to me) was the same as lying. It is called lying by omission. It is deception. Previous to this lesson, "program-goers" warned me that active-alcoholics or (people playing out any addiction) lie. I found this to be true in my case, as well, for obvious reasons. I learned that people-pleasing was a way in which I lied to others. I didn't let people know what I was actually thinking and feeling about them.

Not listening to lies was a new mental boundary that I created with myself, for myself. My mission was to get "off the hook" of his words. Truth was; I was hooked on his words, by his words. The alcoholic's words were like a silky smooth linguistic drug to me.

Promises, "somedays," hope-filled maybes were my "hits." Instead of breathing in those things and taking them to heart, I had to observe his behavior rather than his words — at all times! I had to pull back my narrow focus, my totally involved skewed view of him, and look at things from a larger, more "observational-deck" perspective.

> *"Lack of boundaries invites lack of respect."*
> — *Anonymous*

There were some things that I knew, back then. I saw things with the eyes of maturity, unlike the alcoholic. I knew that a responsible person doesn't leave messes for others to tidy. Likewise, I knew that a grown-up does not leave consequences for someone else to handle. I knew that a trite "I'm sorry" does nothing to repair a mistake in which someone else suffers from – deep in their soul. I knew that apologies were words and amends meant action— like repair and future restraint of similar types of injuries. I knew that if the victim was still stuck having to deal with the consequences of the other person's mistake and offence, then adequate amends had not been made. I knew who was being an adult in this relationship, and who was being a child. I knew how I was being, too.

I read it everywhere, that when we become adults, we become responsible for our own happiness. I learned that regardless of the consequences I was bearing from his violations, the responsibility for my healing transferred to my shoulders. That was a process known quite simply as growing up. Therefore, I knew that any "acting out" instead of expressing my hurt feelings to someone safe was in direct violation of myself, to myself. I had to create boundaries with my pain, and I had to feel it fully and face it. I had to share my pain only with safe people.

I learned that nothing heals as completely as telling the cold-hard-honest--truth. I needed to tell the truth to myself always (in all ways). I often violated my own boundaries, and myself, when I went against my own internal guidance in order to "protect" or save my relationship with the alcoholic. I had to begin to save the most important relationship instead which was my relationship with myself! I had lost trust in myself by puncturing my personal boundaries to avoid the pain of a breakup. I walked all over myself.

Once I got in touch with myself, stayed steady with myself, shaped myself and shifted focus from my outer world to my inner world, I started to get the feeling that my own insides were the best indicator of appropriate limits to set with others. If someone made a request of me that seemed audacious, I needed to say my, "No." Even more basic, if someone hugged me and it didn't feel right, that was all I needed to know. It didn't matter why. I would respect myself. I would stand up for myself.

"I encourage people to remember that 'No' is a complete sentence."
— Gavin de Beckere

Next, I had to act on my own behalf. I learned to pull out of that icky hug and say simply, "I am not comfortable." Furthermore, I had to understand that after I took care of me, I was not responsible for taking care of them or their feelings of rejection. I had to own my limits. I had to set a boundary once a relationship had gone as far as I wanted it to, and I had to clearly communicate by saying so. If I endured unwanted sexual advances in order to placate or hang on to someone else, I injured my own spirit at the expense of not wanting to hurt another's feelings. In acting that way, I wasn't a safe person for me to be with. Those were some of the reasons I couldn't trust myself. I was trying to be nice to others and I was disregarding myself. This was dangerous. Boundaries were needed to keep me safe.

My sponsor would remind me that I couldn't take care of others while taking care of myself. It was sometimes impossible to do both at the same time. Sometimes sponsors are right.

Trust came slowly as I learned my own language, discovered an inner dialogue, and found safety with myself. I became responsible for taking myself out of situations that were less than honorable. I became responsible for avoiding people who used and abused me (no matter how passively the abuse showed up). I saw that I diminished my own integrity by not holding to the limits that would keep me from being exploited, demeaned, or treated with disregard. The alcoholic wasn't the only person I allowed to cross boundaries. It is unfortunate to say that it was my way of being in the world, in order to avoid conflict. I was my own biggest boundary violator.

In recovery, I learned how to show up as a person with personal boundaries. Even if I couldn't explain it or make a good case for it. If I would get a strong internal message to move away from a person or situation, I did myself right by honoring it. Then at a distance, I could talk to someone about it and perhaps be able to verbalize/articulate what was going on. Those were my first steps in trying-out, trying-on, and trusting myself. I practiced picking up on the energy of things, before I was really aware of the dynamic of what was going on. I learned to trust the "energy messages" I received from my own internal guidance system.

With recovery, I even began speaking up. I even dared to speak up when another person's actions (or failure to act) felt disrespectful, thoughtless or uncomfortable. I began to say so (yup, out-loud). I learned that I did have rights to do this. I learned that I do have a say if another person hurts me; my say. I learned that I did and do matter (including most importantly— to myself!). When I employed my old survival mechanism and kept silent, I lost energy, and I lost trust in the relationship I had with myself. I also risked being treated the same way again.

I needed the courage to tell someone that they hurt me. Simple as that. It became similar to calling someone out on their "shit." The active alcoholic didn't like this new behavior one bit. He actually had to go elsewhere, and I understand why now. You can't really live honestly while you're lying. It creates too much internal conflict. No amount of alcohol could wash the truth away.

With my newly established personal boundaries came change. Once, when my alcoholic ex wrote me a note saying that he felt my presence was threatening, I knew I had made good progress with him! Before these bold boundaries (against dishonesty and lies), I used to be such a nice, sweet, and silent doormat that allowed all sorts of unacceptable behavior. Now, I made him uneasy by just standing there in my new shoes. What a great confirmation of my recovery work, I smiled and thought!

In my teens and twenties, I felt confused by how romantic relationships were supposed to work. As I got older and tried relationship tools that were meant to increase intimacy, I learned that intimacy required each person in the relationship be a whole individual. Up to that point, I had used my codependency, sympathy, and empathy to generate intimacy. I focused so much on giving and fixing that I lost sight that a healthy committed relationship included attention from each person TO the other. My experience was that he just took, and took, and took (and took). I never recognized all that taking as neglect of myself in the relationship because I was so damn busy. I kept myself busy. I did know that I was giving, giving and giving, because eventually, I was all given-out.

> *"Givers need to set limits because takers rarely do."*
> — *Rachel Wolchin*

Besides him drinking, our relationship was being neglected by his lack of effort and complete non-interest in couples counseling. I never imagined that absence of adequate attention could be a boundary violation. It was clear to me, even back then, that relationships took work. Why didn't I know that boundaries of intimacy were injured when a mate refused to work out an issue, rejected efforts to repair things, remained coldly aloof, or stayed emotionally unavailable? Those are all actions that create separation. I was learning that a healthy relationship was designed to have certain boundaries that keep safety inside as well as dysfunction outside. What I discovered through studying boundaries was that I had a lot to learn about healthy relationships, and knew very little about boundaries. What I came to finally accept was that I was not in a healthy relationship with the active alcoholic and that made all the difference! Could I stop myself from entering into these types of dysfunctional relationships (by having solid personal boundaries) in the future? Had I grown into my new shoes?

> *"I still have my feet on the ground, I just wear better shoes."*
> *— Oprah Winfrey*

Lesson #17

Beware of Boundary Backlash

Boundary Backlash

"Setting boundaries is a way of caring for myself. It doesn't make me mean, selfish, or uncaring (just) because I don't do things your way. I care about me, too."
— *Christine Morgan*

Why was the alcoholic angry with me now?

I experienced several uncomfortable moments setting boundaries with the alcoholic. On top of that, I experienced after-moments: what I call boundary backlash. It was the thing that happened (the consequence) when he did not like the boundaries I set. Fortunately for my sanity and self-respect, I came to realize that he didn't have to like it! That was the point. The boundary was for me to be safe, respected, and happy, not him. I could not "please all the people all the time." I had a responsibility to take care of myself. There were two lessons my mentors never taught me about setting boundaries; one was that there might be a reaction when I set boundaries with the alcoholic. The second I will get into later.

With every boundary I set, he pushed back. None of his counter-arguments made much sense at all. The issues he created were just reactions on his part. His "push back" was for power and control (both of which he was stripped of when I ended the relationship with him).

My Lesson #17: Brace myself and be
prepared for boundary backlash

I learned that boundary backlash, while unpleasant, was a good sign that he got the message. The message was that I had changed. The message was that I had grown up and I was done being a doormat. I learned to take his attempts to put me down as a good sign that I was on the right path doing the right things for myself. I started to notice that as I made myself happy, he became unhappy. I found it interesting that the tables had turned with my new behavior of taking care of myself. This was a much-needed change for me. How could I take care of myself, if I was always worried about making him happy?

The second thing I was not told was that I, myself, might have a reaction to setting boundaries with the alcoholic. The secondary backlash came from me. Guilt would creep in the back door after I had set a boundary. If I followed-up on this guilt and opted for temporary sanity and quick relief, I would let him off the hook of responsibility again. I also realized that I would be letting myself down again. I noticed the reactionary emotions as a familiar, habitual response of mine, a response that I used to have when I was with him. He would talk in such a way as to elicit and extract this from me. This was how he never got to experience any negative effects of his behavior because I was too darn guilty all the time. I used to backtrack on my boundaries and give in to what he wanted. I learned guilt was a tool that manipulators use.

*"It is necessary, and even vital, to set standards for
your life and the people you allow in it."*
— *Mandy Hale, The Single Woman: Life, Love, and a Dash of Sass*

I fought hard to push through that "guilty-after-standing-up-for-myself" secondary emotion. I felt this "catch-22" all the way through with the help of safe people who would validate my feelings but encourage me to not act upon them. I processed the emotions and analyzed where they came from. I looked back to see the bad pattern of this emotional hold on me and how it played out in my life.

"Individuals set boundaries to feel safe, respected, and heard."
— *Pamela Cummins, Psychic Wisdom on Love and Relationships*

Rather than be the old version of me, I slowed down and applied consequential logic to my guilt. I was willing to try a new behavior and not act on my back-door guilt, no matter how hard it tugged on my ankles and cried "poor me!" I could not give up my fight for sane living. I worked hard to try to be conscious of all my decisions. I mattered now. Everything mattered now, it always had. I worked hard to unearth my motives and act only on the pure ones. I acted only when I had come to a full-term, inner peace with a decision. So, when this guilt would catch me off guard afterward, I had to "sweat it out."

I also took notice of how often my guilt served him and the disease! Not once did this type of guilt serve me and my goals. I knew it would take practice to learn a new external and internal response, but I was up for this challenge. My old ways resulted in more mess and more cleanup. There was no going back on myself anymore, the mess was too big. Self-sabotaging behavior no longer appealed to me as an option to get away from feeling things. I realized that my backlash-guilt was definitely coming from feeling overly responsible for everything and every circumstance. It dawned on me that not all of the problems were mine to handle. So, it was not my responsibility how my alcoholic reacted nor felt about the boundaries I set for myself. They were for me. I learned to brace myself for the inevitable boundary backlash.

I used my own personal tools of "detach and shield" after setting a boundary. I would detach emotionally and mentally, then symbolically shield myself from any anger directed my way. This was the most effective tool. I kept barriers between me and the alcoholic, too. I "bookended" my boundary setting with first a talk with my lawyer, and then, a talk with my sponsor. This was the buffer I needed to set boundaries. Being constantly under besieged by his alcoholism and my codependency required step-by-step support. How else was I going to grow out of this bad behavior of empty boundaries? Were my empty boundaries the same as empty promises to protect myself? Next time, could I be aware that there might be pushback to my boundaries and thereby be mentally and emotionally ready to protect myself again from any backlash?

"I've worked very hard at understanding myself and learning to be assertive. I'm past the point where I worry about people liking me."
— Pam Dawber

The Plight of Self-Doubt

One clear day, my spirit took off and took flight,
that's precisely the moment when the familiar storm appeared.
The dark clouds over-cast my big sky mind,
I began double checking my internal navigation, confusion set in.
Fear of crashing tapped on each of my shoulders like a crazed co-pilot,
Questions raced through my mind, thought by thought,
I entertained each one.
I had no trust in myself, no trust in my ability to fly.
Holding the controls with a sweaty grip,
I called out to flight control towers, no one answered back.
My thoughts reduced to turning around and
making an emergency landing,
I needed external approval and direction.
It was simply the start of this flight,… and my
engines were already running out of gas?
Panic swept through my single pilot cockpit,
That's when I realized the seriousness of my self-doubt.
Was it take off, that set off the doubter within?
Was this an automatic reaction to stepping out on my own,
to attempting to fly my own plane by my own power?
How many times will I land a plane that doesn't need to be landed,
but rather flown through the storm?
How many other souls took inspired action
with an idea, brilliance, genius,
but then stopped at the first sign of dark clouds?
—Grace Wroldson

Stage III

Becoming and Being a Beautiful Butterfly (Taking Flight)

Forgiveness Flies

(Facing forgiveness, feeling whole, and flying free.)

...

"Just when the caterpillar thought "I am incapable of moving," it became a butterfly."
— *ANNETTE THOMAS*

...

"When a caterpillar bursts from its cocoon and discovers it has wings, it does not sit idly, hoping to one day turn back. It flies."
— *KELSEYLEIGH REBER*

Lesson #18

To Forgive or Not to Forgive

My Problem with Forgiveness

"Resentment is like taking poison and waiting for the other person to die."
— *Malachy McCourt*

How could I forgive an alcoholic?

I had a huge problem with the idea of forgiving an alcoholic. Just the thought of offering him forgiveness made me churn inside. "No way!" an internal mechanism screamed out anytime I flirted with the idea of forgiving him. In my agony, it seemed that everywhere I turned, everyone and everything recommended forgiving as the only way to freedom from it all. Logically, socially and morally, I believed that forgiving was something I ought to do. Unforgiveness felt like a sickness that I was swallowing.

Moreover, I was taught somewhere growing up that forgiving was what good people did. So naturally, I also wanted to be a "good person" and get this forgiving done. In my pre-made-up mind, forgiving my alcoholic was the "right" thing for me to do and, I agonized over such a heavy task. Little did I know how wrong I was about what I assumed was "right" for me at that time in my process of recovery.

My Lesson #18: Forgive or don't forgive

After a few years trying, I was flat out frustrated with forgiveness. How was I ever going to forgive an alcoholic? I heard all of the various forgiveness recommendations from well-meaning authors, religious folks, and friends. At one point, I became more than just disturbed; I was annoyed with how lightly they sprinkled "forgiveness-talk salt" on my open wounds. Part of me hoped that forgiving him would naturally happen over time anyhow and so I thought that maybe I would just forget about it until twenty years had passed. Yet, it was still a problem that lingered in the back of my mind. I had a problem with forgiveness.

> *"It isn't that they cannot find the solution.*
> *It is that they cannot see the problem."*
> *– G.K Chesterton*

I read a lot on the subject of forgiveness. Some social experts concluded that forgiveness was a communal act that saves entire communities from falling out with each-other and thus, was a requirement to keep peace and harmony. I longed for that peace for my child and myself. Other newer teachings claimed that forgiveness was a selfish act and recommended that I practice forgiveness of another for the sake of myself. But how? Some famous quotes said that resentment only kills the container it is in, not the other person whom the resentment is directed towards.

One Sunday, I took myself to church to seek a solution for forgiveness. I sat through an entire hour of a Christian service on forgiveness hoping to walk away with a clear-cut answer. The speaker seemed very self-assured, so I was hooked into thinking that she had the answer for me. She was a good Christian mother of four and pointed out that forgiving is something a good Christian does. Again, I heard the same message that forgiveness was a requirement to be a good person. She went on to say that we ought to do it over and over in several different ways. She used eloquent words, made good points, detailed examples, and desperately quoted verses from the Bible. She worked so hard on her speech that she even made the sermon interactive by using a prop. During her sermon, we were all given a little black rock which we took from a basket being passed around the rows. Strangely, it felt nice to pass the basket around and select a shiny black stone. At the end of her speech, she invited all of us to "cast the first stone" if we had never offended anyone or sinned. I sat there in silence looking at my stone in my hand. Needless to say, we all carried our stones home in our pockets. While her well-intended message was indeed nice, informative, and lovingly meant to help us, it didn't work. Something deep down in my gut said it wasn't working for the speaker either. Thus, forgiveness still remained foggy for me.

Unlearning forgiveness

Next, I thought that I needed to clearly define what I thought forgiveness meant. What exactly did it mean after all? After doing some research on forgiveness, I found out that I needed to unlearn my old beliefs about forgiveness first. I was really bogged down with faulty versions. Unlearning old beliefs on this F-word was no overnight skill. For months, I sat around in my head knowing that I had bad conclusions on what forgiveness meant, but I still didn't know what forgiveness was.

"We fail more often because we solve the wrong problem than because we get the wrong solution to the right problem."
– Russell L. Ackoff

What about acceptance instead?

Then, on my quest to be free to finally forgive, I unexpectedly stumbled on a healthy forgiveness alternative. I was filled with relief after I got up. I became entirely ready to try out this other creative concept. Carrying unforgiveness around for so long was heavy, and it felt heavier each year. I was tired and very motivated to let things drop and to move forward with my life. My little black stone from that church service was placed in a bag on my back which was hard to lug around. The alternative felt authentic, satisfying, and more real than forgiveness. I found a new solution for my problem with forgiveness, and it was called acceptance.

Acceptance felt to me like the energetic equivalent to forgiveness. Acceptance was a great healthy alternative in my case because it did not involve pardoning the offender nor condoning the harm done. I knew that learning this healthier option would take some time for me to integrate. In my situation with the alcoholic, I had to replace forgiveness with acceptance. I was so relieved that this finally made sense to me. I felt as if I had been set free from my "forgiveness problem." I would accept what happened in the past instead. I would accept what the alcoholic did and didn't do and still validate my own reality of the hurt and pain I suffered. This felt like my truth.

For myself, I found out that forgiveness does not mean:

✧ forgive to forget,
✧ forgive and allow the same bad behavior,
✧ forgive and let the person off the hook for what they are responsible for,
✧ forgive and take the person back into my trust,
✧ forgive and release the person to harm me again

I vowed to myself to unlearn those popular and people-pleasing sayings and ideas.

Is an expectation a premeditated resentment?

At one New Year's Eve party during my foraging for forgiveness, I listened to party-goers reflect on their year. I was stunned to hear a woman say that she didn't have much forgiving to do last year. Wow! Impressive. Wait? What?! The women went on to explain that she had recognized that forgiveness was the result of her own personal expectations being unmet. Huh? She explained that she had done a lot of work on her bad habit of creating expectations and therefore found herself having to forgive less. What a concept! Was it true? Could I stop expecting things from the alcoholic and myself and thus have to do less forgiving?

> *"If you are unable to understand the cause of a problem, it is impossible to solve it."*
> *– Naoto Kan*

Seeing my part

In my mind, and on my mental scoreboard of life, I personally mapped things out. I made a mental timeline of all the supposed transgressions of the sick and suffering alcoholic and when offenses had happened. Did an expectation precede each forgiveness struggle? Admittedly, I had tough egoic-obstacles to push through. It wasn't easy to "see my part" in the problem. It wasn't easy to get past my pride and victim stance. However, if I went back far enough, I found that indeed this was true! Forgiveness had everything to do with my expectations of my ex (the alcoholic) and what he should and should not have done.

Forgive myself?

Furthermore, I found the same issue with myself. I was struggling to forgive myself because I had expected better of myself in the past. I had decided I ought to have been better, smarter, stronger, etc. I came to realize that the only reason I needed to stretch so hard and

111

reach so far for forgiveness was because I had expected myself to not succumb to the disease of alcoholism and codependency. I had expected better from myself. What was I expecting, perfection from myself? I didn't fully understand that I, too, was human. In recovery, I was now learning how to be human and humble.

When I unearthed my expectations, I found some really alarming ones. I had expected that my ex would be a much better person to me after breaking up. (Huh? But Yup.) I had expected that my ex would be a much better person than the behavior he demonstrated when I was pregnant. I expected that, when I became a mother to our child, I would get a certain type of special respect from him. But how wrong I was in all these judgments! How very off the mark! I had let myself expect better behavior, action, and thoughts from myself and my alcoholic. I came to learn that we were who we were at the time. This includes wounds, unconsciousness, pain, confusion, and all of the other ingredients that become part of a person's past. At that time, we weren't able to do better than we were doing.

When I took an honest and often frightening look at myself, I came to see that judgmental, faulty thoughts passed down through generations and society was in-part to blame for having the heavy burden of trying to forgive. It was judgment that got me into trouble. I heard someone confirm this once saying that "children blame and adults take responsibility." How astonishing to realize that it was actually an error in thinking that caused all of my agonizing problems with forgiveness. This was very much a maturity issue as well. Once I understood this, I was able to move forward with my own forgiveness process. I finally felt like I was taking steps in the right direction to fully heal. These new ideas felt true to me. I could accept things instead of focusing on forgiving the alcoholic's selfish acts. I could release my expectations. I could invite awareness into my thinking. Maybe I could even, eventually, forgive?

> *"Everyone says forgiveness is a lovely idea,*
> *until they have something to forgive."*
> — C. S. Lewis, *Mere Christianity*

Lesson #19

Come to Forgive Yourself

Offering Myself Forgiveness

*"I have learned, that the person I have to ask for
forgiveness from the most is: myself."*
-C. JoyBell C.

Could I ever forgive myself?

My first move toward forgiveness

My first authentic move toward forgiveness had to be self-forgiveness. I needed to begin with myself. How could I forgive the alcoholic when I hadn't forgiven myself? This was yet another area where I placed the alcoholic first in my life. UGH! How embarrassing to realize that after all this time, I was still focused on him! I needed to *again* take the focus off the alcoholic and put it back on myself. How could I extend pardoning behavior to someone when I myself was completely mad and disapproving of my own actions of the past? How could I forgive myself for not being wiser and more aware? How could I forgive myself for judging myself so harshly, thinking that I ought to have been stronger than the active disease inside of him and me? How could I have possibly done better with the company I kept, and the lack of knowledge I had at the time? I couldn't have done better or I certainly would have.

My Lesson #19: Come to forgive myself

Forgiving myself was my next right step. I needed to find compassion for my struggle and accept that I could not win the losing battle of an alcoholic relationship. If I thought about all the things that tormented me, I knew I had a lot to forgive. I had expected and wanted so much more from myself than I was able to actually deliver (at that point in my life). I was at my bottom when I made my worst, personally "unforgivable mistake."

Before really practicing recovery, my life was rolling on year after year, but with active disease festering. Little did I realize that as his alcoholism progressed, so did my personal battle with codependency. I progressed to being "diseased minded" myself. Things that I said I would never do became things I comprised on and actually did. I too had gone down and lowered my standards, so as to not have to let go of the relationship.

I heard it said that forgiveness is of the past, not in the present. And by the time I approached forgiveness work, I had a lot of past to deal with. I had a past full of decisions centered around staying with the alcoholic, all at the very costly expenses. The expenses included my own soul, goals in life, and my true desires. I felt loss and grief, knowing what I could have done with my life if I had only let go of him when I should have. I finally started to see the cause of my own pain – me. I was unable to let go.

Silent forgiveness

Before I knew about the option of acceptance as an alternative to forgiveness, before I knew that I needed to forgive myself first, I was side-tracked. I spent years working on forgiving the alcoholic. When I felt like I had failed at forgiving him, I tried to practice a version I called "silent forgiveness" of him, because I no longer wanted to carry around the pain and hate in my mind, body, and soul. I decided that if forgiveness was for me, then why should he even know about my decision to forgive him? I felt that forgiveness was a very personal decision. I thought I had found a clever way to forgive (for me) and was planning to keep the act of forgiving him all to myself as a way to complete the task and heal. At the time, this felt like an accomplishment. I had no idea that I was trying to forgive quickly so I didn't have to feel the depth of my pain and grieve more loss. Also, I had no idea that I was trying to forgive quickly because it was actually a bad habit of mine. I wanted to "get along" because I was afraid of confrontations. I didn't even realize that my alcoholic never ask for my forgiveness in the first place!

For almost a year, I prided myself on my "silent forgiveness" method and praised my efforts. I told myself that I could only reach this point when I no longer needed the un-forgiveness to protect me from more harm from him. I felt like I had done a good job in the self-protection department. Originally, not forgiving him kept the pain real enough for me to never let down my boundaries again.

In my journey out of the alcoholic relationship, I had set up plenty of walls, banned him from enough parts of my life, and kept that maintenance program going strong. I no longer needed an angry "unforgiveness stance" to protect myself from further disease-laden harm.

In my attempt to accomplish some forgiveness, I went on a retreat to explore forgiveness, mistakenly thinking that after a weekend of setting an intention, by being willing, and by loving myself, I could be forgiven forever and completely healed. What I discovered was that acceptance, rather than true forgiveness, was what I needed to be working towards instead. On retreat, I was able to identify different kinds of forgiveness. Who knew forgiveness came in so many flavors? I found some unhealthy versions I was well-practiced in. One was a quick type of forgiveness and the other a complete non-forgiveness. With the alcoholic, I had tried both and failed at sustaining those brands.

I also explored what Real Forgiveness required. I came to believe that Real Forgiveness required the other person to seek it and want to help in the healing process. This meant that the offender had to "tough it out" and make it through an amends process. My ex didn't want this type of forgiveness, nor was he willing to make things up to me. In his narcissistic, self-centered mind, he believed he did nothing wrong. He was too wounded and incapable to care for (or about) my wounds.

Living amends to myself

I began to learn about the new healthier definition of genuine, authentic forgiveness. Immediately, I knew that I could apply this to me rather than to him. I wanted forgiveness. I was willing to make apologies to myself. I was willing to make living amends for the harm done. I knew that I was worth it. I was willing and wanted to be a partner in my own healing.

"It's toughest to forgive ourselves. So it's probably best to start with other people. It's almost like peeling an onion. Layer by layer, forgiving others, you really do get to the point where you can forgive yourself."
— Patty Duke

Before I could make any progress, I needed to release my perfectionist view of forgiveness. I wanted to believe that if I did forgive myself once, it could be done and last forever. I also believed I had to do this wholeheartedly and completely. What ended up working for me was doing this process gently, and allowing it to be a gradual release. I embraced it as a lifelong, loving process. I also embraced this as forgiving myself in percentages and increments. I also made allowances for relapse into unforgiveness of myself. For example, when my life got hard, I would hold myself in contempt of what I previously thought was a crucial bad choice: having a child with an alcoholic.

How much was I responsible?

"The more you know yourself, the more you forgive yourself."
— *Confucius*

By realizing how much I had to forgive myself for, I was able to clearly see my emotional health as an issue. Originally, I felt 110% responsible for my child's existence and life. I felt like a horrible mother for bringing her into a family plagued by alcoholism. I eventually came to share that responsibility with a Higher Power, her father, family history, society, and other factors beyond my control. When I did this, I could forgive myself because I decided I was no longer fully to blame for the past. I could take a small portion of responsibility for my role in her life and go forward doing a better job for her.

I also began to get an accurate picture of how much forgiveness work with myself was effective by claiming a percentage of forgiveness. On some of my issues, I was able to offer myself 50% forgiveness, while with others I was only able to offer myself 10% forgiveness with a pardon for simply not knowing better. I worked towards increasing, little by slow, just how much I wanted to forgive myself. I became willing to see things in a different perspective to assist me with this gentle process. Beating myself up with unforgiveness hurt. I ultimately had to decide to forgive myself, even if it meant that all I could get to was 80%. My ability of forgiveness at the time had to be good enough. What other choice did I have if I couldn't fully forgive myself?

*"There is no sense in punishing your future for the mistakes of your
past. Forgive yourself, grow from it, and then let it go."*
— *Melanie Koulouris*

I was willing to offer myself forgiveness in small amounts, which
meant I was capable of loving myself a little more. I would be a
participating partner in the apology and reconciliation to myself
which I needed for further healing from his disease of alcoholism and
my issue of codependency. My issue caused me so much suffering.
Ceasing to suffer over self-contempt and unforgiveness of self was
work I could do something about. It was "my side of the street" that
I could clean up.

I could be more compassionate to myself and more understanding
of my wrongs. I could communicate a new language of love to
myself, letting go of the past mistakes and recognizing them as
growth opportunities. I could gain new perspectives on my troubles.
I had tools and abilities while in recovery that I didn't have available
to me while in active disease. My new abilities gave me hope. I could
now apologize to myself. I could now show myself with action; I
was now going to love myself going forward. I asked myself, "could
I forgive myself a little bit more with each act of making amends to
myself?"

"Forgiveness is a gift you give yourself."

— *Suzanne Somers*

Lesson #20

Practice Peace,
Detach with Love

How I Left

"I said to my soul, be still, and wait without hope
For hope would be hope for the wrong thing; wait without love
For love would be love of the wrong thing;"
— *T.S. Eliot, Four Quartets: East Coker*

How shall I leave an alcoholic relationship?

I had a choice in how I left the alcoholic. I contemplated for months how I could leave the relationship in a way that would grant me the most peace and give me closure. I knew so well that I was prone to relapse, often forgetting all the unacceptable behavior, and then passively agreeing to get back into the toxic dance with him. My old choices included leaving him with red-hot anger, which always provided enough rocket fuel to eject me from a relationship. Or was there a way to leave with peace and gratitude? Even if he left me (my easy way out), I would still need to do the work of leaving him in my heart, mind, and soul. Basically, I still had to do the leaving.

My Lesson #20: Leave with peace, let go with love

I knew there were several important stages in decision making. One therapist explained to me that I was stuck on the wheel of the decision-making process. My wheel was perpetually stuck on the rock of pre-contemplation and not moving around. Staying stuck in pre-contemplation was a subconscious stalling tactic to any momentum that would get me away from him. Eventually, I had to deem myself knowledgeable enough, willing enough, strong enough, and equipped enough to act on my behalf and leave. It became time to do the work and move my wheel. It became time to take action when the pothole of pity was getting too deep, and I was feeling like if I didn't act, I'd be stuck forever. I prayed to my Higher Power to send me a spare.

I had to re-remind myself that my decision to leave was not about him; it was for me and my health. The breakup would no longer be punishment for him not doing what I wanted, being what I wanted, or for screwing up. Leaving would now be a gesture of self-love. I found that deciding was an action quite opposite of keeping this problem in my mind. Keeping it locked in my mind and not taking action on my own inner guidance was becoming unfortunate for even me to witness never mind my friends who were wondering what was taking me so long to make my move. I had to make a decision then act accordingly. I prayed nightly to my Higher Power for help with this.

Then finally, at long last, after years, after many relapses, after knowing his disease patterns intimately, after learning about myself and my weaknesses, and at the relief of myself and my soul, I decided that I didn't want to hurt anymore. I decided that this was my last round and my bottom: I would go no further with this relationship choice. I had undoubtedly gained enough wisdom and lessons from crossing paths with the disease (and walking side-by-side, chained to it), that I didn't want to hurt him anymore either. There were ways that I finally began to see how I too inflicted pain. I inflicted pain in various ways that seem subtle and kept me seemingly self-righteous. I partook in enabling drinking, caretaking like a mommy, yelling like a teenager with a temper, undermining him, sarcasm, manipulations, silent treatment, pouting, spilling beer on him, and other passive aggressive behavior to get my needs met and anger out. I didn't like this about me. I could no longer fool myself.

By practicing loving-kindness and patience with myself, I calmly made the choice of how I would leave him and exit the alcoholic relationship. I recognized that it was in my best interest to do so carefully, with full consideration of myself and what I was going to take with me. I had a choice on whether to take the good or the bad memories (or both). I had a choice to let things go or carry them with me. This meant not only things, but memories, emotions, hurts, lessons, gratitudes, and blessings.

Detaching with anger

Still reeling from anger over the last betrayal, I decided to sit tight for a few months on my bottom and allow the big emotions to pass until I had some type of inner peace. I learned how anger could be useful for keeping me away from re-engaging with him. I learned it was that wonderful signal emotion indicating that I allowed him or myself to cross a personal boundary. Anger was oftentimes useful in giving me the power leave him, however, what it didn't do was help me detach.

Oh, Anger. Anger was the explosive jet fuel that propelled me on many-a-crisis out of my entanglement with the alcoholic, who was being overruled by the disease. However, it was not the best fuel that ever sustained my decision. Anger would wear off my heart, and I began softening with time and compassion. Then my mind would forget the pain! If I ended it with anger, anger followed me. It did because it was in me. It provided me reasons and justifications. I always had a lot to sort out and make peace with after I would jet off. I sometimes allowed anger to consume me in a blaze, and then it left me in ashes. I am not saying that I didn't learn a lot about myself by that method of breaking up. It certainly had its advantages and challenges. My job was to do the necessary resolving within and come to inner peace then leave.

Detaching with love

Ultimately, I wanted pure, clean, loving detachment. Detaching with anger left me chronically angry. I heard that detaching with love would leave me loving. I wanted to end up being the loving person I knew I was, so I practiced detaching while I was still with him. Each day, I practiced detachment. I had to detach from my dreams, hopes, and visions with him to finally reach some acceptance and peace. I am sure he felt this.

Detaching with gratitude

I came to know that detaching with full inner peace with the gift of understanding left me in a state of more permanent peace. I know that this peace was powerful enough to prevent my yearnings for another round of "relationshiping" with an alcoholic. I had tried many early attempts to detach with just gratitude as a way to appreciate my journey with him in the past and honor those memories, lessons, and moments. Friends encouraged detaching with gratitude because they claimed it helped to cultivate a state of appreciation and grace that I would bring into my next relationship. At the time, I was unable to see any next relationship. All I could see was him and my overwhelming heartbreak and grief. My next relationship came in the form of a relationship with a Higher Power, my soul, and myself.

How I leave is how I begin again

Now, I see the wisdom that how I leave is how I begin my next journey with someone. After a few relationship attempts after the alcoholic, I have come to know that just because I can't see the anger I started with the next man, doesn't mean it didn't show up in the relationship. My issues were under my unhealed, resentful surface just waiting for another reason to be angry at "the new guy," especially if he turned out to be like the alcoholic in any way. Leaving in anger left things unresolved within me – every time.

I came to the conclusion that I was worth a new clean beginning. I believe there comes a time in everyone's life when you realize you are worth having something good in this journey. Then I came to believe I was worth it and I owned it. There came a time when I had acquired through tears, agony, and pain a peaceful heart about my decision to leave.

I had learned enough lessons

The final choice and the chance to leave the relationship came from a beautiful place of peace and love. When I left the relationship in the past, there was unrest, uneasiness, fear, and unresolved guilt. That was when I must have needed to stay and learn more with the alcoholic. However, I became very sick repeating lessons and doing more learning. Mostly I became emotionally ill. This included fatigue and tiredness of learning the painful lessons he brought to me. I had a final thought: I had learned enough with this man. Anger in that thought was useful, it let me know that I had had enough of this. However, my final thought was a vision of me waving a white flag.

Grace W. Wroldson

Healthy choices

At some point, the decision in my mind to leave the relationship became simpler and less complicated. It came down to simply making another healthy choice on my behalf. This is how I "stepped-up" in my life and started taking good care of me. This way I didn't have to endlessly find reasons to make him wrong. I also didn't have to justify my wanting to be healthy and happy. My mind really wanted to prove I was right in my decision and action. The obsession with trying to be right was that I had to always make him wrong. For that, I suffered what I call "after-guilt." I would feel bad about making the alcoholic bad (in my mind).

My mind was a trickster. My mind often engaged in self-doubt and then backflipped and found reasons that I was wrong, too. What if there was no wrong or right? What if it was simply a choice? What if it became a choice I made with genuine understanding and a true peaceful heart? How much lighter would that feel?

So I made the lighter and healthier choice. Making my decision to leave can be boiled down to just a choice in that present moment to retain my sanity and surround myself with healthy things. Negative things, like active alcoholism, had a guaranteed way of rubbing off on me when I was around them, so I made a choice about which things I wanted to rub off on me. Choice became easy when I measured it up against healthy versus unhealthy. What I discovered to be great about choice is the chance to choose again at any point. Even with that tool, I always kept in mind that would from now on choose in my own best interest, not his.

"It's choice — not chance — that determines your destiny."
— Jean Nidetch

Being grateful to let go

Being grateful helped me let go. I took my forgiveness and reflections of my lessons learned. I found that I could even be grateful for the toughest lesson with him even lessons of jealousy, envy, and everything else I learned about me. He contributed to me expanding my self-awareness. There were moments and experiences that I still treasure with his soul. There were good times to remember before the progressive disease debilitated them. However, nostalgia was not going to make me go back and get hurt again. I could resist because I had peace. Leaving in peace and gratitude was the best way for me. It was a better stance and had better energy to carry me forward. I listed all the things I was grateful for with the time we spent together. Those were beautiful memories I cherished as I grieved the active end of this relationship.

Turning him over

After detaching with love, after making peace with the past, after practicing gratitude, I then (in my heart and mind) turned him over to his Higher Power. I finally understood that what happens to him is up to him and his Higher Power. I concluded that the alcoholic is equally loved by a Higher Power. Was it now time to turn myself over? I wanted to be loved.

> *"I shall be telling this with a sigh*
> *Somewhere ages and ages hence:*
> *Two roads diverged in a wood, and I—*
> *I took the one less traveled by,*
> *And that has made all the difference."*
> — *Robert Frost, The Road Not Taken*

Stage IV

Flying with Brilliance and Grace (Dancing the Dance of Life – From a Higher Altitude)

(Moving on, practicing gratitude, and living a life of freedom.)

...

"Just living is not enough," said the butterfly, "one must have sunshine, freedom, and a little flower."
— *HANS CHRISTIAN ANDERSEN, The Complete Fairy Tales*

...

"Only those who stick around long enough to see the caterpillar turn into the butterfly actually get to witness the transformation."
— *KRISTIN MICHELLE ELIZABETH*

...

"When she transformed into a butterfly, the caterpillars spoke not of her beauty, but of her weirdness. They wanted her to change back into what she always had been. But she had wings."
— *DEAN JACKSON*

Lesson #21

Move On

When the Alcoholic Moves On....

"If someone is not treating you with love and respect, it is a gift if they walk away from you. If that person doesn't walk away, you will surely endure many years of suffering with him or her."
— *Miguel Ruiz, The Four Agreements*

What do I do now that he has another woman?

When the alcoholic moved on, I learned to let him. A friend of mine told me, "don't trip him up!" Part of me wanted desperately to go running back to him and that old, familiar relationship. In my heart, I knew that that would certainly "trip him up" because I broke it off the last time, and his ego would surely love to say to me, "I told you so." However, I learned that when a person walks away from me, I must let them go, or I will probably endure many more years of their suffering, as well as my own. I knew this was the truth. I knew instinctively from all the history between us that this would be the case. Nobody had changed. However, my heart was aching to hold onto him. I tried to tell my heart that we couldn't go backwards. Yet, my heart at the time kept recalling all the wonderful memories, good times, and unyielding passion, to send to my brain which emotionally distorted my thinking. I was grieving, and I finally had to face all the loss.

> *"You and you alone are responsible for dealing with your own pain. This is your program of recovery."*
> — *in a suggested Al-Anon welcome*

It was reiterated to me that I am responsible for dealing with my own pain and this meant I couldn't call the alcoholic to make him share in my pain and misery. How many times did I put that task on him? I used to call him to let him know how much I was hurting. Before solid recovery, I always let him know. Instead, this time, I hung onto myself, my recovery and my soaking wet pillow for many nights, in pain. I fought and accepted the change and loss, and it gave me new strength; I had made it through, all by myself.

My Lesson #21: I must move on, too

I was anxious at the news of a new woman even though I had prepared: physically I lived on my own in my own apartment; mentally I had done so much reading on the disease; emotionally I received the support of many well versed friends and from therapy; and spiritually I started relying on a Higher Power for those really intense feelings such as trauma, depression, and despair. I had prepared for the day when he would come to tell me with some kind of honesty, that he was moving on and that the promise of his happiness was being found in a new woman. But, I knew better. He wasn't happy to begin with, and I learned that oftentimes we get from a relationship what we bring to the table.

I had made peace knowing that I could not live in such close proximity to this active disease – that I could not be happy with him. So, why did it still hurt so much to find out that there was another woman so soon? Was it because I let my emotional sobriety slip a few weeks ago and shared a tender moment with him before he came clean about her? Did I expect loyalty from him still? Was it because he claimed that he wanted to respect the new woman and give her the honesty and self-restraint and the happily ever after that I never got from him? What was I crying about? Was it jealousy, pain, loss, self-doubt, fear of abandonment? Or was it all of those things?

I had to realize that sharing a tender moment with him was a way that I had let my emotional sobriety slip. It set me up to be vulnerable with him again. Engaging in self-pity, self-contempt, and self-doubt was also what I called "slips" in my recovery. My fears of missing out, or "FOMO" as I refer to it, on a happy life with him came back to visit me with his news. Even after all my hard work in letting go, apparently, my heart still had specks of hope for a divine reuniting. The anxiety of not choosing to be with him and trusting myself was almost as strong as my anxiety of being with someone I did not trust – him. I was forced to face my intense feelings. I was afraid to feel. Panic would set in the moment I realized I was about to feel that wave of grief and all of my scary feelings again. This nocturnal panic over my lost love happened often at night, and I tortured myself with visions of him happy with the new woman. It was a bad pastime.

> *"When people can walk away from you, let them go. It doesn't matter how attracted you are to them, how wonderful they are, whether they did you a huge favor years ago or what the situation is, if a person can walk away from you then let them walk."*
> — *T.D. Jakes*

With all my tears and walking around in a shell-shocked state, I started to get better at understanding that pain is inevitable but that the suffering part is optional. So, why couldn't I shut off these re-runs and silent conversations in my mind? Why was I losing sleep when I knew the day would come that he would have a new woman? In all my worst-case scenarios, the "new-girl-fear" came up when I planned my departure from the relationship. I had prepared to let go and to be at peace with the possibility. Yet, after finding out about her, I wondered how much longer would I have to endure my pain over them? I even wondered if I should just divert my attention to a new love (for me) to get some romantic-relief myself? Would going out with someone new cheapen the love I had with him, if found someone new, too?

I had come to learn that a rebound was a rebound. I always felt that it was not fair to the unsuspecting party – the new person. And, I never felt very good afterwards about using others or being used for that type of healing, or distraction. I choose not to do this method of recovery. I knew all the facts of rebounds; I did the right thing by myself, and I cried and cried, night after night. I lost precious sleep with our new baby beside me, and, again, I felt so sad and so alone. I was definitely healing by facing all the pain, and I was giving myself the gift of time to feel my feelings – all of them. I needed more healing. I needed more self-love, not romantic love. I needed more of myself. I needed to get through. I needed, and I did. I grieved. I got strong. I got through. I moved on during the year they were together which was also the same year that they broke up. Was this a surprise to me? Did I think he had great, long-lasting relationship skills? And then I stopped myself and asked, "wait, did I have any great relationship skills?"

> *"When people walk away from you, let them go. Your destiny is never tied to anyone who leaves you, and it doesn't mean they are bad people. It just means that their part in your story is over."* — *Tony McCollum*

Lesson #22

Seek Solutions for Yourself

Self-Solutions

*"We can't solve problems
by using the same kind of thinking
we used when we created them."*
— *Albert Einstein*

I wondered... how do I solve problems with an active alcoholic?

We had problems. As a matter of fact, the alcoholic and I had many problems. We had one problem after another. We had problems that couldn't be solved. We had problems that lasted. We had new problems every day, piling on top of the old problems. To my dismay, there seemed to be no permanent solution for the endless problems we faced. That is until I started recovery, and I "let it begin with me."

*"Running away from a problem only increases
the distance from the solution."*
– *Anonymous*

When I let change begin with me, it certainly did create new temporary problems. However, the problems shifted from all

133

"strapped to my back," to his problems that he created for himself. I needed to build a solid sense of self and to learn to practice self-solutions, for those were my only effective solutions from which I benefited.

Over the years, it became clear to me that he couldn't solve his problems. Unfortunately, my sense of over-responsibility caused me to continually step in (unasked) and try to help. I stepped in even after the final separation and breakup. Strangely, I stepped in even when we were on separate teams in a court battle. I thought helping him would help me and our child. I thought I could be his translator for how the world works and for how he could keep from getting in trouble with the law. His problems became my problems only because I made them mine.

So, as it unfolded, my problems began to overwhelm me because most of the problems weren't mine to begin with. I was trying to fix things that I didn't break. I was trying to do his rational thinking for him. I was using my brain power to think for this unconscious and "off-line" active alcoholic. My solutions didn't work for him because my solutions were only for me.

My Lesson #22: My solutions are for me

After my mental exhaustion and many breakdowns, there came a day when I made a decision to stop making up solutions for the alcoholic and seek solutions for me instead: to deal with him. I needed to learn to cope. His disease wasn't going away, and I was not going to abandon our daughter to this disease. I had to get self-focused self-solutions and let him sink or swim. In my past, I was way too relationship focused. Did I even look at my problems with money and self-doubt?

When there were only problems all the time, I would sometimes sink into hating the fact that I had a child with an alcoholic. More truthfully, I was depressed that I had allowed myself to get pregnant with a sick and suffering alcoholic, who wouldn't and couldn't show up for me in a healthy cooperative way. With this child, I would be on my own, all alone and worse... tied to him and all his problems. Mostly, my feelings were a mix of self-loathing, self-pity, and self-resentment. All the years I spent in Al-Anon, hearing other women's stories, let me know that it was not fun (and sometimes disastrous) raising a child with an active alcoholic. The pregnancy meant I was tied to him, having to deal with him and his alcoholism, even though I left the relationship. When my thinking slipped into a self-pity party, I felt like I ruined my life and my future. It felt dangerous to me, to be bringing an innocent, vulnerable child into a world where she might be around such an ill father. When I ended the relationship, I wanted complete detachment from him and the horrid disease from which he suffered, but that's just not what happened. I had to accept the fact that I walked fifteen years into the relationship and then needed to walk fifteen years out.

As our child grew up, it's not surprising that we were unable to co-parent together, due to his opposition and problems with things like honesty and communication. I needed an alternative, so I began parallel parenting instead. I did what I thought was best, as her primary parent. I shifted my entire focus to focusing on me. I worked on becoming the best parent I could be, doing what I thought was right. I parented without his support or cooperation. The alcoholic did whatever he wanted because he was going to do that anyway, despite all my efforts to warn him of the possible dangers of court, law enforcement, and child protection agencies. Needless to say, I used my lawyer and child protection agencies often.

In his illness and issues, he couldn't see the amount of money being spent on court and lawyers, and how cooperation rather than his pride would have left us all with more money and more peace. He was unable to see past his anger and resentment that I left him during my pregnancy and to his dismay he had responsibilities to fulfill according to the courts (i.e. our child and child support payments). The chief enablers in his life enabled court battles to continue, year after year. I realized, at one point, that if it weren't for his enablers, he would have failed long ago in his self-destruction and possibly sought help or changed. They say that approximately four people get sucked into the vortex of an alcoholic, for us it was twenty-one and counting while we went through the court processes. I saw clearly as the years passed, as he continued to be an active alcoholic, that the disease of alcoholism was still in my life, even though I left the relationship.

At times, I would believe that there was no chance of his getting help while his enablers felt sorry for him, or me, for that fact. It was hard not to allow resentment to poison me when court continued on. I was human, and there was a lot that I could be resentful for. I found it interesting when some of the court motions I resented, later became blessings for me. Always being the defendant paid-off in the long run. Looking back, I wished I welcomed every court motion as a gift instead of viewing it as a curse. How much happier would I have been through it all?

I learned to accept what was happening. I finally had to seek solutions for myself against this disease of alcoholism. I had to have protections in place for me and my child. It was the same thing as my discoveries with setting boundaries. I would set a boundary, and he wasn't able to respect it. Eventually, I had to set boundaries with just myself and honor those continually. So, it went with solutions too: I had to focus on solutions that led to my serenity. So, my solutions couldn't involve finding solutions for the alcoholic. The depth of his problems became clear to me when he had fought and won in court the exact parenting schedule he wanted, the exact requests granted, and yet he still was unhappy with the final twelve-page agreement. Thus the alcoholic's problems continued. It was then that I decided to stop trying to make him happy.

I needed to accept that his continual unhappiness would lead us back to court time and time again (as long as his enablers enabled him). I needed to file complaints and modifications of my own and seek a schedule that worked for me and my child and forget about his requests. I had to again say "No" to him via lawyers and stand for what I wanted. I had to forget trying to appease the alcoholic who wouldn't be happy with anything because he didn't have the ability to be contented. Disease does that to a person.

Sometimes, I had to wait a year before taking action toward a solution for myself. Things got easier when I learned to let go and turn the problems over to a Higher Power to solve. Some of our troubles I couldn't contend with, they were way more than I could manage. I also learned to lift these problems up in prayer and do nothing about them by any Earthly means.

The bottom line became that I had to find solutions for myself, rather than find solutions for the confused alcoholic. Most of my solutions became court solutions, where a judge would enforce them because I couldn't enforce anything. I had to enforce things with myself like self-disciplined boundaries. I had to stick to my solutions, myself, because I could enforce those! And, often, I had to reinforce them!

> *"Not everything that is faced can be changed.*
> *But nothing can be changed until it is faced."*
> *– James Baldwin*

When I grew stronger and more self-serving, he became angrier and angrier. This triggered fearful reactions in me which I learned to breathe through and get help. I had my worries over how this mess would impact our child, but I recalled the hope in the saying, whispered in my ear on an Al-Anon Spiritual Walk, that "if one person gets better in recovery, the whole family benefits." I was willing to allow all of them (the sick alcoholic and his team of enablers) to blame me for all the mistakes, and know that this was not my fault as our custody went further into an expensive court battle. I could see that they couldn't see. I came to know that I was not wrong. I learned to be strong and accept the attacks being directed at me versus a much worse scenario of the "disease of blame" being taken out on our child. I was mature enough to accept the fact that he and his enablers were holding me responsible for his disability. They say alcoholism is a family disease. I found compassion for all the players in this litigation, including myself. Court agreements, eventually accomplished safety for me and my child that I could not have done on my own. There were many positive sides of court. I came to see the good it did for me.

From my view, the alcoholic didn't learn the lessons. Sadly, it was as if he couldn't learn in the ways that one would hope or expect. He learned more manipulative tactics, and how to take his problem to another new woman rather than learn how to be healthy first. He could not solve his own problems effectively. His short-sightedness led him into more temporary agreements and legal fees, to simply put in black and white what each parent must do. In a normal situation, these trivial matters would be understood as things to compromise on and negotiate about. Not an active alcoholic, however! Not him! There was no normal, rational, nor cooperative living in his vocabulary, yet. Our situation appeared more and more abnormal to the courts and to the judge as our file grew larger and larger. It became more complicated as I spoke up and out against unacceptable behavior. Mostly, I just "hung in there" and hung on. I said my prayers and remembered to be thankful. Going to court was one of the ways I learned to be confident and strong against this adversary.

> *"All problems become smaller when you confront*
> *them instead of dodging them."*
> *– William F. Halsey*

I recognized that court became a self-esteem issue for him, which I could never solve. My self-esteem began to increase with every "esteemable act of courage" to care for myself and our child. There was a power transfer that happened when I worked my program of recovery. I stopped being so afraid of court appearances; I learned to accept them as part of our story. Ultimately, the court protected me and my child from the alcoholic in countless ways.

I checked my motives as time went on and learned some of the deeper reasons I had for trying to create so many solutions for him. I realized that I worked so hard because I wanted, craved, and longed for peace. I didn't want to feel uncomfortable, unliked, nor afraid of what his family would think of me. No matter how nice I was to him and no matter how much I allowed, his family couldn't see the true cause. On the one hand, they may never know how lucky they were to have a woman like me to raise their grandchild. They could only feel sorry for the alcoholic and afraid for him, just as I was afraid for him to continually make mistakes or hurt our child. I saw him burning bridges and not understanding the consequences of his risky, unstable behavior. But no matter what he was up to, I had to focus on how to stabilize myself, physically, emotionally, mentally, and spiritually. I made the switch from solutions for him to solutions for me.

What was my solution to my self-resentment? It was self-forgiveness. What were my homemade solutions for my situation? First, I shifted my perception of a "ruined life" to a life filled with the joy and blessing of a beautiful child who was my ultimate reason for working the Program and changing. She was my angel and hero. Without my deep-seated motherly instinct to protect her from this disease, I might have gone back to the alcoholic many more times. Then, I kept the intermediaries in place that established a buffer zone for me that protected me from any verbal abuse and attacks. I documented everything possible. I worked with my lawyer. I stayed in recovery and utilized my sponsor daily. I sought supports for every problem. I focused on myself. I went to counseling. I took time to de-stress. I educated myself. I stopped blaming myself. I stayed cool, calm, and collected during court appearances. I got honest. I practiced self-care and let others call me "selfish". I loved myself through all the grief and pain. I focused on myself. I obeyed the laws. I honored the agreement. I looked and appeared reasonable to a judge. I took the focus off him and put the focus back on me and my healing. I journaled about all the insights I gained. I wrote. I savored my awarenesses. I reached out to other strong recovery friends with situations. I worked on my control issues and fears of confrontations. I prioritized good sleep. I exercised by walking a mile every day. I took time-off and time-outs. I followed up with my own health issues. I focused on myself. I practiced meditation. I read about alcoholism, love addiction, and codependency. I took yoga classes. I prayed to a Higher Power. I made new friends and nurtured my other friendships. I took good care of myself within this challenging situation of raising a child with an alcoholic. I found solutions that led to my serenity, not his. Could I outgrow my problems this way?

> *"Sometimes problems don't require a solution to solve them;*
> *Instead they require maturity to outgrow them."*
> *– Steve Maraboli*

Lesson #23

Live a Saved Life

Living as Saved

*"When we long for life without difficulties,
remind us that oaks grow strong in contrary winds
and diamonds are made under pressure."*
— *Peter Marshall*

How do I live without the alcoholic?

At the very of my bottom of my bottom, I had spent half of my life trying to save the alcoholic and my relationship with him. It never occurred to me to save myself. I never valued myself the way I valued the relationship with the alcoholic. I forgot about me daily, while obsessively thinking of the relationship and him. When my years of recovery began to work in my life and the exact moment that my focus finally broke from him to me, I was saved. I went from trying to fix him to healing myself. I gathered the loved I had for him and applied it to myself, and that made all the difference!

After the pain filled years of trying to save the alcoholic relationship, there came a day that I finally woke-up to the realization that I had to just save myself. This realization turned into my mission. I had to save myself from his sinking ship and sail away. That's when my next work began. That's when my next, new, better life began. It was all about me now. The self-honoring thing to do was to live as if I had just saved my life because truly I did!

My Lesson #23: I have to live like I just saved my life

I had to learn how to live my new life, which was now all about me and taking care of myself. Self-focus and self-care took practice. I had to learn to live as "saved." I spared myself from the close-up viewing of the progression of the disease of alcoholism. Even more so, I stopped the deterioration of myself and spirit. It felt like a complete rebirth, and it took a while for me to adjust to living saved. It's odd to admit this, but it took years for me to live comfortably without the alcoholic relationship. Breaking codependency habits are like breaking an addiction.

My new life was much, much quieter. I enjoyed the peace. It was a simpler life where joyful moments could be found while mothering my child. I caught myself laughing again as time went on. For so long, when I was active in the thick of the alcoholic relationship, I struggled. I was so focused on making it through and hanging on. In that relationship, I was simply surviving and parts of me and (my dreams in life) were dying. All of that grief had to be processed. That also took healing years.

My new relationship work involved self-approval on an hourly basis and many self-affirmation statements written on my mirrors. I discovered that serenity and sanity were wonderful to experience and worth hanging onto. I was on a personal honeymoon with myself after letting go of the alcoholic and learning to love myself. After self-saving, I then had to self-partner.

When I first opened this gift of a new life, I wanted every woman to have this freedom from a toxic, alcoholic relationship. But I soon learned that this gift was only mine to keep. Other women in similar situations had to find and fight for theirs. No matter how hard I tried, I couldn't give other women mine, and I couldn't coach them into theirs. After a few attempts at trying to save women like myself, I learned that things like courage, self-love, and fearlessness only come from within when a woman is ready and fully supported by herself. Even though I believed every woman had it in them, it was still theirs to empower. It was up to them to practice their version of recovery and life after an alcoholic relationship. I could only set a good example. I knew that I could to be an inspiration to them as I lived on and moved on. That was when I knew I had to not only write but publish.

I will admit, in a busy world, it took me a while to get used to the slowed-down pace of life without the alcoholic entertainment. Silence was unsettling at times with a less chaos and drama-filled existence. It took years to get used to life, the new way, the recovery way. It took a while to enjoy my own company. Adjusting to my new alcoholic-free lifestyle, I became able to enjoy things that I was never able to fully enjoy before.

For the first three years, every day after the separation and detachment from his disease, I woke up with tears of gratitude saying, "thank you so much that I do not live with active alcoholism anymore!" I thought I was saying a thank you prayer to God, but then realized I was also thanking myself.

When I learned at the break of my bottom that my co-dependent soul sickness was seriously affecting my life, I learned to also say, "thank you so much that I do not live with active codependency anymore! Please keep me clean." I had to learn to live with the new me. I always recall my bottom moments. Sharing about my bottom has been a valuable tool that I use to live a "saved life."

Once free, I observed how different I was on the inside as the results of my "recovery time." Years ago, I would have agonized about being alone, living alone and choosing alone. Not anymore! I was happy to be free of him and my troublesome attachment disorder. Even more so, I felt free from having to protect myself psychologically from both his disease and mine. It was refreshing not to be in a state of constant stress. I understood that I had survived and that I needed the rest, the reflection and a rebirth.

I still had to practice self-protection trying to co-parent with the alcoholic, but my stress wasn't to the same extent as the previous several years of trying to break free. I had put firm boundaries in place. Now, I could just monitor the combined problem (the disease which would love to have me roped back into enabling and my issues which fed off an internal reactionary drug-store) around the alcoholic. I began to learn healthy ways to entertain my boredom and keep the focus on my healing.

After surviving twenty years of a relationship with an alcoholic, it has been important to me that I acknowledge to myself that I survived the disease. I was living "The Promises" of recovery now. I was self-approving of having left him. I affirmed myself for my numerous, new, healthy decisions. I enjoyed living with positive thoughts originating from my own mind. I had even arrested my own addictions – to being right, people-pleasing, saving, rescuing, fixing, love addiction and codependency. I wanted to hang onto this miracle with all my might. He didn't get recovery, but I did.

I still had my battles with internal fear and some PTSD from the pain of the alcoholic relationship. Sometimes I was so afraid that my thinking would relapse to wanting the alcoholic back (for quick, temporary relief) that I would plan ahead and put safeguards in place to help prevent "slips." I knew that I was hanging on for my life now. I hung onto my health dearly. I finally felt worth it. I finally felt that life was worth it.

I came to see that living as saved would take full-time consciousness, dedication, awareness, and work. My work towards self-love came but it was quite awkward at first. Self-love was a new "norm" that needed to be implemented so I could grow comfortable with it. It didn't matter how uncomfortable growth was, I knew I had to do it. After so much of my youth lost to loving an alcoholic, I was eager and happy to start my new job of loving myself. Living saved became a practice of grace and gratitude. I felt like I had given myself a second chance at life. I switched into self-saving mode with a mission of self-preservation. I was now acting on guidance with and without fear.

I had learned so many valuable life lessons through my experience of loving and leaving an alcoholic. After examining my painful past thoroughly, which I acknowledged was the precursor to my present, I had so many amends to make to myself. There was considerable "clean-up work" to be done, some of which took years to accomplish as amends to myself. Some of that work came with long hand-written apology letters in my journal – to myself. Most of my sincerest apologies to myself had to be in making active, living amends, where every day, I made up (to myself) for all the self-abuse and self-doubt that led me back under the alcoholic's control and into my sickness.

After setting myself free, I made up for missing out on my life by going after my dreams, my goals and my hopes for me (all things I once had). After terminating the relationship, I finally had energy for these things. Energy came rushing in because I had cut ties with my alcoholic (the best I could) and went "NO CONTACT." My life filled with wonderful friends, activities, interests, work, and love. How nice it was to finally have energy for me again! This became my every day in recovery with myself, the Program, and my Higher Power. I hiked a new path in grace and with grace. This sweeter life was on the horizon for me, I only had to let go of his heavy backpack and climb my own mountain. I had to fully embrace myself, do the work, and focus on me.

In the early stages of my change, I had to ask for a lot of outside help and support – so I did. My appreciation for even the simple things grew as my life grew better and better. My tears were of thankfulness for my beautiful daughter, genuine friends, and my loving, kind, compassionate self. I was grateful for myself. I liked me again. I liked who I became. Others began to notice that I loved myself —this was because I finally remembered myself. I remembered the miracle of me. I rescued myself. I saved my life. How do I live without the diseases of alcoholism and codependency? I live free.

"Her words are her wings. She's flying."
– A.D. POSEY

Lesson #24

Practice Gratitude
(And be filled with Love, Light, and Appreciation)

-A Journal Entry-

"Start seeing everything as God, But keep it a secret."
—*HAFIZ*

What if my situation with the alcoholic never changes, is there still a way for me to have peace?

October 3, 2017

Letter to the Alcoholic,

This is a thank you letter from my soul. It marks my growth, wisdom, and maturity. It's not the typical thank you letter that one writes when one is treated well and is appreciative. It's a thank you for the mistreatment that led to many insights, awarenesses, and discoveries. It led to a surge of character that mounted within me. It caused me to turn and face another monster besides you and the disease of alcoholism – me and my codependent love addiction. My journey with you turned out to be a hero's journey of changing my circumstances and healing the terror within me. Life was not happening to me, it was happening for me.

First, I will acknowledge that I can recall some beautiful times we shared with our mutual love of nature. For those experiences, I feel the traditional sense of gratitude of having your company. I think it is something of an accomplishment to have met each other in high school and to have witnessed our growing-up process (or not growing-up issue) over twenty years, into the people we became. I, launching into the woman I am becoming, and, you, into the man you are becoming (or will continue to be). I now let that be up to you. I have learned that people don't change until they have a reason to change. I was surprised to learn that I was not your reason and that you were not mine. I found change to be an inside job (not about outer circumstances) and most importantly, a choice. I chose to change.

I am grateful for our mutual blessing, our child. She has been my greatest teacher and biggest love and joy on this earth and in my lifetime. I see that she is a part of you and a part of me. I don't deny that anymore. How privileged we were to hold her as an innocent baby, watch her take her first steps, and learn to talk and say our names. Now, we watch her grow into this brilliant and beautiful precious little girl we know. We also get to watch her make mistakes, just as you and I have had to do. Lucky for us, we both were able to experience being parents, even if separately. And, separately, is what I am very happy about now. I feel enlightened on that issue.

I see that she is happy to have both her mother and father living and in her life. She cherishes each of us as a loving presence in her life, as we cherish and adore her. I love being called mom. And I love hearing her call me "mommy." Those are such sweet words to my ears from her young little voice. And those are the words that remind me of my responsibility to her. A responsibility to keep her safe, not just from the disease of alcoholism, but also from the various forms of codependency I could engage in if I was not active in my recovery. I strive to stay conscious, daily.

I have come so far. The road I traveled with you was bumpy and at spots broken-down. I have learned many valuable lessons on the bumps. For me, I have learned how to love properly by not loving in a healthy way, by making mistakes. Equally important, was when I learned to let go. It is now seven years ago, that I consciously made a decision to let you go after our lengthy journey together to save myself and my sanity. I am thankful that I let go for both of our sakes (actually for all three of us). No one was kept prisoner. Our relationship was dysfunctional and harmful to each other. I am glad we both walked away. Our daughter doesn't need to see the ugly side of our human struggle. She doesn't need to watch our suffering played out as we bump into each other. We can pass on our wisdom or our woe onto her. I choose wisdom. She can hear about us as a story when she is older. She can learn how I overcame it all and what it took. She can be spared from a diseased, disorderly life. She has a chance.

We had our chance and dance. I am in awe of the beautiful flower that came from our mud. We co-created this special child, and I feel she was sent from God as a small but powerful savior. I have found contentment by letting you go to live your life and evolve separately. I believe that this has been for our highest good and the best interest of our child. She gets to see me at my best and you at yours, without each other's pain getting in the way of her life. I fought hard for her so she wouldn't see us fight.

It seems hard to believe that I have discovered many hidden treasures of you dragging me to court as many times as you did. Your anger with me kept our child under constant supervision and protection from the disease of alcoholism. That is something that I could not do single-handedly as a single mom. I see now the benefits of overcoming bitterness and anger. You gave me plenty of practice speaking up for myself, a skill that I needed to learn in this lifetime. Court did not defeat me, it strengthened me!

I am uncovering the blessings of you as my first original "qualifier" into a Twelve Step Recovery Program. My care/concern for you, landed me in the program of Al-Anon. My love for you kept me there long enough for me to understand that I am my own "qualifier." The program of recovery has shielded both me and our

child from more pain and needless suffering. The bottom line is —
she has not had to be raised in an alcoholic home because I got the
help that I needed. She has been immunized by the disease, and I
work hard to protect her from any further harm and uncertainty that
the disease and the co-disease manifests. She has enjoyed a relatively
stress-free pregnancy to gestate in as well as a six-year stable home
with me, as I seek help with assistance programs in order to not have
to live in dysfunction with you. I know she would thank me if she
knew all this and if she could. Someday she might.

I wake up every morning filled with gratitude to be on my own
and free. I go to bed every night peaceful without anxiety and fear
over anyone's destructive drinking or thinking habits on my mind.
I thank myself and my Higher Power daily for that gift of peace.

You, I can thank you for being the rough edge that smoothed
me out and polished my abilities. I built strength and courage that I
didn't know the coward codependent in me had. Thank for pushing
my buttons and pushing me into the Program. I also can thank you
for participating in our daughter's life to the best of your ability.
This includes a thank you for staying out of our lives when you
did. Thank you for fighting in court so that I could see who you
really are more clearly. You continually reminded that you are a sick
and suffering person and this kept me away. Thank you for not
asking me back and moving on with your life to the next woman.
And thank God that I did not go back to our toxic relationship
when I found out I was pregnant. Thank you for all your "acting-
out," because it made me work on my issues and find my worth.
Thank you for showing me who I wouldn't want to marry, as I now
found someone I would want to marry. Thank you for the loneliness
your absence brought out when you abandoned me while pregnant
because I found a loving Higher Power to fill that void. My Higher
Power walked in when you walked out. Thank you for reneging on
responsibility, since it forced me to rely on God and learn to lean
into God's more powerful presence in my life. I am not afraid to use
God or the word "God", anymore.

Thank you for the laughter of our youth. Thank you for the tears of a broken heart that helped me water and rebuild my hope. Thank you for your company in nature, as I continued on to find it to be my special place to retreat, reflect, and renew— without you. Thank you for the sorrow you left behind and the memories, for those were my teachers of self-compassion. I will cherish yesterday, dream of my better tomorrows, and live for today.

As it turns out, I was able to survive the family disease of alcoholism and reclaim my life. I was able to protect, love, nurture, and nourish our daughter's little soul with all I had to give. I did this with recovery and all without your diseased-interference and the times you tried to intervene. I am able to approve of me now since I don't need you for that. I came to love myself since I don't need you for that either. I began caring for me, because you didn't or couldn't. I now know that I will get better and better without you. I am now, more able to help and serve others in an authentic and inspiring way. Thank you.

My Lesson #24: Practicing gratitude fills me
with love, light, and appreciation.

Lesson #25

Ask Yourself, Did You Learn the Lesson?

The Butterfly Effect

"Chaos is nothing more than beauty about to dance."
—AD POSEY

What's in a name?

I have been a witness to my own butterfly effect (in my life) as the result of learning my lessons. The butterfly effect is a scientific theory that explains that a single occurrence, no matter how small, can change the course of a universe forever. My universe has certainly been changed by the small changes I made within my thoughts. It's the notion that a butterfly fluttering on one side of the world can impact another part of the world through atmospheric-like changes. As my changed thoughts fluttered, the atmosphere of my mind began impacting my beliefs.

The butterfly effect phenomenon helped explain how small changes, within the complex system of my mind, had such large effects that played out in my life. My new beliefs impacted how I lived my life. I made new choices as to where to fly. I took my new mind out into the world and it created my new life.

It became important for me to label the changes that I underwent. I named them so I could claim them — so to speak. By naming the lessons and reviewing what and how I learned with a clear head, I was able to keep the knowledge alive in my awareness. This was the alchemy of my life transition. I was able to spin straw into gold. I took my painful lessons and spun them into golden wisdom. My wisdom was for me to wear like new clothes, or new wings, in my new life. There is a popular saying about taking leaps of faith that I lived by to get me through gaps. Because sometimes, I jumped and hoped my wings would appear!

> *"Leap and the net will appear."*
> *— JOHN BURROUGHS*

A few well-intentioned friends who were committed to certain spiritual teachings and trains-of-thought claimed everything was just pure Love and warned against naming disorders – like labeling my alcoholic an alcoholic. They warned me not to label any person or I might mistakenly lock them into an unmovable position in my mind. Name-locking, they claimed, would not lead to healing for either person. They believed my labeling the alcoholic would hold him in a place and hold him in a perspective where he would not be treated with the love and respect that every human being deserves. They claimed it would not allow for change. And I partly agreed. I could understand how that could happen if someone was not aware of the disease of alcoholism and hadn't heard all the sharing happening in the meeting rooms on compassion and dignity. Throughout my life, I have come to learn that everything has both aspects. Labeling was helpful for me because it helped me to identify the problem and look for solutions that apply. I respected their wisdom, and so, I have always remembered to make room for change and new titles – like recovering codependent.

By using labels, I knew what topics to research and get specific help with. Al-Anon was specifically for my situation because the title of the program fit my description. I was dealing with what looked like a real addiction brewing in him, and I was dealing with real codependency issues arising in myself.

Putting a name to the drinker and the myriad of dysfunction by calling him an alcoholic helped me remember who and what I was dealing with as the chaotic years went on. Identifying myself as a codependent and love addict helped me know just who I was dealing with when BIG EMOTIONS took over my logical mind. My love issues and abandonment fears had to be named and claimed. I needed to label myself and the alcoholic in order to look clearly at myself and my situations. Labels held things in place that were often too psychically subtle to catch onto, so I could catch on. That was how labeling helped me.

My Lesson: Label the lesson, write it down!

What also helped me emotionally was "separating the person from the disease." I didn't allow the label to make my vision so black and white. I only would let the label help me in my research for finding the right tools to get a healthy solution. When bad behavior was happening on his part or mine, it was a mental skill that I had to acquire to pull the person who was suffering away (in my thoughts) separate from the outward behavior. I needed to remember that sometimes we all can get buried under our issues in times of stress or when triggered. When triggered, my early traumas tended to come up and take over unless my recovery was strong enough to stop me, then catch me. I found that the self-love solution brought me back to wholeness, every time. My healing mission wasn't about labeling him an alcoholic, it was about remembering that he was more than an alcoholic, he was a person, and he was suffering too. I needed to label both myself and him in order to identify the key issues and to get the right doors open for help.

So, with all these lessons and labels I was giving myself help. I was giving myself what I needed to learn. I was teaching myself about my life and discovering my learning style. When I told my sponsor, I was writing down the lessons to actually learn them, my sponsor jokingly asked me, "well, did you learn the lesson?" to which I replied, "several times over!" Laughing at myself was part of the joy of my recovery. Laughing with others in recovery at some of the silliness of codependency (holding it as a separate pattern within good people) and its funny way of trying to work in our lives, was a sign of a healthy understanding, forgiveness, and true humility. I could see myself as separate from my "codependency slips." My labels weren't about pinning myself down or putting me in a hole and becoming the label I had given myself, it was about remembering that it was part of me, but not all of me. It was a way for me to identify the things I needed to overcome, to fully heal, and to be healthy.

Lesson #25: Ask myself, did I learn my lesson?

When tough situations came up, I learned to ask myself if I had learned the lesson from before. Recalling was crucial whenever I had to confront the alcoholic or my triggers into codependency. Before I would start my old ways of reacting (poorly), I could catch my codependency right before by remembering the lessons and calling my sponsor. I learned my lesson, and, thus I didn't have to repeat the pain.

"I long to accomplish a great and noble task, but it is my chief duty to accomplish small tasks as if they were great and noble."
— HELEN KELLER

Living with lessons changed me. If I had been a rose, tight in a bud from my fears, I had only just opened to my beauty to love myself and others from a good heart. If I had been a very codependent caterpillar, I had broken down and reformed, to breakthrough as a butterfly. If what I was doing in my life before recovery was crawling, I had taught myself to soar.

If all of my brokenness in relationships was part of a journey in my life towards putting myself back together and to become whole again, recovery had pieced me back together with each lesson. Wisdom wove me into the quilt of who I became and who I wanted to be. If I had partnered with the alcoholic to learn the lesson of the need for self-partnering, I learned to shake my own hand and commit to myself. If my life had been a dance, I had an alcoholic dance partner long enough to learn to enjoy dancing alone to new freedom songs of my spirit. If this had all been about the journey and not a quest to a destination, this butterfly learned to stop and smell the roses and sip the nectar. I also learned that not all lessons were painful. So, what other lessons did this beautiful life have to teach me?

"Similar to a butterfly, I've gone through a metamorphosis, been released from my dark cocoon, embraced my wings, and soared!"
– DANA ARCURI, Reinventing You: Simple Steps
to Transform Your Body, Mind, & Spirit

When Truth Resonates Within You

When truth resonates within you,
You hear it, you feel it, you know it
Awareness hits you like a giant unannounced ocean wave,
Then washes over you as you stagger to regain your footing,
All your senses alert, align, awaken
Truth rings a bell with an invisible tone,
Truth sends a loud unseen vibration,
Truth opens a window of fresh, cold, breathable air
Then your face softens, to an expression of awe and wonder
Your thinking tumbles for a moment,
like underwater sands sifting through the streams of thoughts,
Finally, your mind opens and drinks in the clarity of the message,
Your soul savors the sudden moment,
when that clear, direct signal reaches the deepest part of you,
Your hair drips droplets of denial,
as you walk off the beach,
That's the moment of truth,
When truth resonates within you.
— Grace Wroldson

My Final Blessing to You

May you be free.

...

"Just like the butterfly, I too will awaken in my own time."
— *Deborah Chaskin*

...

"We delight in the beauty of the butterfly, but rarely admit the changes it has gone through to achieve that beauty."
— *Maya Angelou*

The Meaning of the Blue Morpho Butterfly

An Emblematic Symbol

"Change can be beautiful; butterflies are the greatest proof of this."
—*Matshona Dhliwayo*

Butterfly Brilliance and a Full Metamorphosis

Do you see the butterfly in you?

Captivating, the Blue Morpho butterfly is a brilliant, magical symbol of transformation. They have shimmering blue, iridescent wings which have a very special and unique diamond-shaped structures that reflect light. Blue Morphos are lovers of the light and are meant to fly within the sunshine of this Earth. These butterflies capture our attention and serve as a symbol of endurance, change, hope, and life.

Strikingly beautiful on the outside, these particular butterflies have multiple predator defenses. The underside of their wings is secretly camouflaged in order to help them blend-in with plain colors of browns. When they close their wings, they avoid becoming prey. When in flight, their wings appear to flash from vivid blue to dull brown as they glide through the air. Thus, the butterfly seems to continuously disappear and reappear again, making it very hard to track (another great feature of their built-in ingenuity to survive). They inspire us to practice not just grace, harmony, and beauty, but also self-preservation, self-defense, brilliance, and the power of reflecting and living in the light. Their unique journey from the ground to the sky amazes us. When they, fly we stand in awe.

The butterfly metamorphosis represents the magic of getting a second chance at life and of living at a higher altitude. This can be associated with raising our consciousness, connecting to a Higher Power, and living in a thriving state of gratitude and blessing. Butterflies have long been associated with a deep, powerful representation of the soul as well as spiritual transformation. The caterpillar changed form so significantly that it outgrew life on the ground and flies free above it. What an amazing evolution!

As an animal totem, this magnificent creature is considered sacred, mysterious, and spiritual. The journey from caterpillar, to chrysalis, to butterfly, symbolizes the coming of age (to a mature, free-flying adult). Morpho butterflies complete an inspiring transformation. Are you ready to transform yourself - and your life?

"Any transition serious enough to alter your definition of self will require not just small adjustments in your way of living and thinking but a full-on metamorphosis."
—Martha Beck